BARRON'S BOOK NOTES

WILLIAM
FAULKNER'S

The Sound and
the Fury

BY

Elsa D.

SERIES COOR.

Murray Bromberg
Principal, Wang High School of Queens
Holliswood, New York
Past President
High School Principals Association of New York City

BARRON'S

BARRON'S EDUCATIONAL SERIES, INC.

ACKNOWLEDGMENTS

Our thanks to Milton Katz and Julius Liebb for their advisory assistance on the *Book Notes* series.

© Copyright 1985 by Barron's Educational Series, Inc.

All inquiries should be addressed to:
Barron's Educational Series, Inc.
250 Wireless Boulevard
Hauppauge, New York 11788

Library of Congress Catalog Card No. 85-3943

International Standard Book No. 0-8120-3541-0

Library of Congress Cataloging in Publication Data

Dixler, Elsa.
   William Faulkner's The sound and the fury.

   (Barron's book notes)
   Bibliography: p. 111
   Summary: A guide to reading "The Sound and the Fury"
with a critical and appreciative mind encouraging
analysis of plot, style, form, and structure. Also
includes background on the author's life and times,
sample tests, term paper suggestions, and a reading list.
   1. Faulkner, William, 1897–1962. Sound and the fury.
   [1. Faulkner, William, 1897–1962. Sound and the fury.
   2. American literature—History and criticism] I. Title.
II. Series.
PS3511.A86S835   1985   813'.54   85-3943
ISBN 0-8120-3541-0

CONTENTS

CONTENTS

ADVISORY BOARD

We wish to thank the following educators who helped us focus our *Book Notes* series to meet student needs and critiqued our manuscripts to provide quality materials.

Sandra Dunn, English Teacher
Hempstead High School, Hempstead, New York

Lawrence J. Epstein, Associate Professor of English
Suffolk County Community College, Selden, New York

Leonard Gardner, Lecturer, English Department
State University of New York at Stony Brook

Beverly A. Haley, Member, Advisory Committee
National Council of Teachers of English Student
Guide Series, Fort Morgan, Colorado

Elaine C. Johnson, English Teacher
Tamalpais Union High School District
Mill Valley, California

Marvin J. LaHood, Professor of English
State University of New York College at Buffalo

Robert Lecker, Associate Professor of English
McGill University, Montréal, Québec, Canada

David E. Manly, Professor of Educational Studies
State University of New York College at Geneseo

Bruce Miller, Associate Professor of Education
State University of New York at Buffalo

Frank O'Hare, Professor of English and
Director of Writing
Ohio State University, Columbus, Ohio

Faith Z. Schullstrom, Member, Executive Committee
National Council of Teachers of English
Director of Curriculum and Instruction
Guilderland Central School District, New York

Mattie C. Williams, Director, Bureau of Language Arts
Chicago Public Schools, Chicago, Illinois

HOW TO USE THIS BOOK

You have to know how to approach literature in order to get the most out of it. This *Barron's Book Notes* volume follows a plan based on methods used by some of the best students to read a work of literature.

Begin with the guide's section on the author's life and times. As you read, try to form a clear picture of the author's personality, circumstances, and motives for writing the work. This background usually will make it easier for you to hear the author's tone of voice, and follow where the author is heading.

Then go over the rest of the introductory material—such sections as those on the plot, characters, setting, themes, and style of the work. Underline, or write down in your notebook, particular things to watch for, such as contrasts between characters and repeated literary devices. At this point, you may want to develop a system of symbols to use in marking your text as you read. (Of course, you should only mark up a book you own, not one that belongs to another person or a school.) Perhaps you will want to use a different letter for each character's name, a different number for each major theme of the book, a different color for each important symbol or literary device. Be prepared to mark up the pages of your book as you read. Put your marks in the margins so you can find them again easily.

Now comes the moment you've been waiting for—the time to start reading the work of literature. You may want to put aside your *Barron's Book Notes* volume until you've read the work all the way through. Or you may want to alternate, reading the *Book Notes* analysis of each section as soon as you have finished reading the corresponding part of the original. Before you move on, reread crucial passages you don't fully understand. (Don't take this guide's analysis for granted—make up your own mind as to what the work means.)

Once you've finished the whole work of literature, you may want to review it right away, so you can firm up your ideas about what it means. You may want to leaf through the book concentrating on passages you marked in reference to one character or one theme. This is also a good time to reread the *Book Notes* introductory material, which pulls together insights on specific topics.

When it comes time to prepare for a test or to write a paper, you'll already have formed ideas about the work. You'll be able to go back through it, refreshing your memory as to the author's exact words and perspective, so that you can support your opinions with evidence drawn straight from the work. Patterns will emerge, and ideas will fall into place; your essay question or term paper will almost write itself. Give yourself a dry run with one of the sample tests in the guide. These tests present both multiple-choice and essay questions. An accompanying section gives answers to the multiple-choice questions as well as suggestions for writing the essays. If you have to select a term paper topic, you may choose one from the list of suggestions in this book. This guide also provides you with a reading list, to help you when you start research for a term paper, and a selection of provocative comments by critics, to spark your thinking before you write.

THE AUTHOR AND HIS TIMES

William Faulkner once said that *The Sound and the Fury* began with a picture in his mind. Four children, a girl and three boys, are playing in a stream near their house. They have been told to stay outdoors, although they don't know why. In fact, their grandmother, who has been very sick, has died, and the grownups are holding a funeral. The girl, more adventurous than her brothers, climbs a tree to catch a better view of what's going on in the house. Watching her from below, the boys notice that she has gotten her underpants muddy.

Why was that image—which appears in Benjy's section of *The Sound and the Fury*—so vivid to Faulkner? Perhaps it reminded him of an important incident in his own life. Like Candace Compson ("Caddy" for short), Faulkner had three brothers. And like the Compson children, Faulkner called his own grandmother "Damuddy." She was his mother's mother and died when he was small.

The Sound and the Fury is not the story of Faulkner's life. But it contains many places and people Faulkner knew. Jefferson, where the Compsons live, is much like Faulkner's hometown of Oxford, Mississippi. Like the Compsons, the Falkners (an ancestor had dropped the "u" from the original family name, but William Faulkner put it back) were one of the oldest and most distinguished families in town. Faulkner's mother, like Mrs. Compson, came from a family that was not quite as distinguished, and she never forgot it. But Faulkner's father, like Mr. Compson, was a hard-drinking, bitter man, who couldn't live up to his family's past.

Family, place, and past. These things were most important to William Faulkner. After he was five years old, he and his parents lived only a few blocks away from his grandfather's home, The Big Place. Faulkner's grandfather was a successful lawyer and businessman. Townspeople called him the "Young Colonel" even though he had never served in the army. Faulkner's great-grandfather—like the Compson children's grandfather—fought in the Civil War. Nicknamed the "Old Colonel," he commanded the Partisan Rangers, guerrillas who attacked Northern troops behind their lines. The Old Colonel wrote novels, too. One of them, a murder mystery called *The White Rose of Memphis*, was a bestseller.

So it isn't surprising that when the Young Colonel's oldest son became the father of a boy, he gave him the Old Colonel's first name (William) and the Young Colonel's middle name (Cuthbert): William Cuthbert Falkner. Although the Old Colonel had been dead for eight years when his namesake was born in 1897, he was still alive in the memories of Oxford and of the Falkner family. No wonder that when his third-grade teacher asked Billy Falkner what he wanted to be when he grew up, the boy replied, "I want to be a writer like my great-granddaddy."

Their pride in the Old Colonel made the Civil War very real to the Falkner family. The war still affected everyone else in Oxford, too, even though it had ended in 1865. Its most important effect was on relations between blacks and whites. As a result of the Civil War, black slaves were freed, but most got little more than freedom. They generally could find work only in white people's fields or as servants in white homes. Except for a few years right after the war, they could not vote. Segregation laws, passed only a few years before Faulkner was born, prevented black children from attending school with whites, or from riding the same railroad cars or entering the same churches or stores. So, although many blacks lived in Oxford, the only ones young Faulkner knew were his family's servants. The housekeeper, Caroline Barr, was a second mother to Faulkner and his brothers, who called her Mammy Callie. She served as the model for Dilsey in *The Sound and the Fury*.

Faulkner was a quiet, dreamy boy. Despite his interest in reading and writing poetry, he dropped out of high school. His only real friend was Estelle Oldham, and he was sure they would marry some day. But Estelle's family wanted her to marry a graduate of the University of Mississippi. Although Estelle loved Faulkner, she gave in to her parents' wishes.

Estelle's marriage affected Faulkner deeply. He decided to join the Army in 1917, just as the United States entered World War I. But the Army rejected him because he was too short. Pretending to be British—that's why he put the "u" back in the family name—Faulkner talked his way into the Royal Air Force and was sent in 1918 to Toronto, Canada, for training. The war ended before he even flew a plane. However, Faulkner came back to Oxford with a slight British accent and a limp he called a battle injury. He then enrolled as a special student at the University of Mississippi, taking courses in English and French literature.

Eventually, Faulkner dropped out of college, too, and took odd jobs to support himself while he wrote poetry. Many of his poems were about Estelle, who by now had children and lived in the Far East. Encouraged by a friend, Faulkner sent his poems to magazines, and they began to be published. He lived briefly in New York, where he worked in a bookstore. But the city he liked best was New Orleans. He spent time there, getting to know other writers and artists, and wrote *Soldiers' Pay*, his first novel, there.

During the 1920s, many American writers went to live in Paris, where they could live cheaply and be part of the exciting experiments there in writing and painting. The American writers Ernest Hemingway and F. Scott Fitzgerald lived there. So did James Joyce, the great Irish novelist. Joyce pioneered a new technique of writing called stream-of-consciousness. Instead of describing what a character was thinking, like most novelists, Joyce put the character's actual thought process on paper. Joyce's approach had great influence on Faulkner, who spent 1925–26 in Paris and traveling around Europe. Then Faulkner returned to Oxford and to New Orleans and continued writing.

By now Faulkner had turned thirty and hadn't yet established himself as a writer. He had published several novels, but they hadn't sold well. Neither Estelle Oldham nor another woman he'd loved had wanted to marry him. He could barely earn a living. But within a couple of years, his life turned around. In 1929, Estelle divorced her husband and married Faulkner. *The Sound and the Fury*, his fourth novel, was published later in the year and some people called it a masterpiece. Magazines began to buy Faulkner's stories, and with the proceeds he bought an old mansion, which he called Rowan Oak. He lived there with Estelle, the two children of her first marriage, and several black servants. Faulkner and Estelle's own daughter, Jill, was born in 1933.

Faulkner's novels continued to receive good reviews, but he couldn't make enough money from the books to support his family. So he followed a number of other American writers to Hollywood to work on film scripts. Faulkner never liked Hollywood, but he made enough money there to pay for life at Rowan Oak. Faulkner's reputation continued to grow, and some people said he was one of the best American writers. In 1950 he won the Nobel Prize for Literature, probably the highest award for a writer. Faulkner was only the second American to be so honored. Sinclair Lewis, author of *Babbit* and *Main Street*, had been the first.

In the 1950s, black Americans, especially in the South, stepped up their struggle for the civil rights so long denied them. At first, Faulkner supported them. As you can tell from reading *The Sound and the Fury*, Faulkner respected black people. Dilsey keeps the Compson family together, and she and her sons are both stronger and warmer than the white people in the novel. In some of his other books, like *Absalom, Absalom!* and *Go Down, Moses*, Faulkner even said that the guilt for slavery was a curse that would destroy white Southerners.

As the years went by and the civil rights movement achieved some success, however, Faulkner backed away. He said blacks deserved equal rights in American society but needed time to prepare for them. He advised black leaders to move slowly. He wrote that Mississippians should integrate their schools voluntarily, because integration was right. But if the government forced them to admit black children, he would resist. Not surprisingly, black leaders were disappointed in Faulkner, and black writers denounced him. Yet, Faulkner gave some of his Nobel Prize money to local black schools, and he sent several black youngsters from Oxford to college in the North. He was capable of helping individual blacks but couldn't understand why blacks would need a political movement to win their rights.

Faulkner died in 1962, following a fall from a horse, although the long-term cause of death was his lifelong alcoholism. He never saw the bloodiest years of the civil rights struggle in Mississippi nor the movement's eventual triumph.

Faulkner left a great body of work, which included 19 novels, and is considered one of America's foremost writers. He said that *The Sound and the Fury* was the book that caused him "the most grief and anguish," and his feeling for it resembled that of "the mother [who] loves the child who became the thief or murderer more than the one who became the priest." Perhaps because *The Sound and the Fury* drew so heavily on emotions associated with his own childhood, its writing opened floodgates in Faulkner. Afterwards "I said to myself, now I can write," he recalled.

And write he did. Most readers believe Faulkner's earliest novels—*Soldiers' Pay, Mosquitoes,* and, to a lesser extent, *Sartoris*—are much less interesting than the ones that followed *The Sound and the Fury*. In the year after he finished it, he completed two other novels, *Sanctuary* and *As I Lay Dying*. (Although *Sanctuary* was written first, it was not published until 1931, a year after *As I Lay Dying*.) *Sanctuary*, a dark, bitter novel about corruption and the middle-class hypocrisy that supports it, was the first of Faulkner's books to gain wide popular attention. *Sanctuary* resembles *The Sound and the Fury* in its pessimism and identification of female sexuality with evil. *As I Lay Dying* resembles *The Sound and the Fury* in other ways. It, too, is the story of a family—the Bundrens, poor Jefferson people attempting to bury the mother. Like *The Sound and the Fury*, *As I Lay Dying* is technically brilliant, using several narrators to tell its story. Only a year after the publication of *Sanctuary*, Faulkner completed *Light in August*. A story of emotional isolation, set in Faulkner's imaginary Yoknapatawpha County like *The Sound and the Fury*, *Sanctuary*, and *As I Lay Dying*, *Light in August* focuses on racial problems.

The publication of *Light in August* marked the end of Faulkner's first creative period. Later books like *Absalom, Absalom!* and *Go Down, Moses* further explore the South. *The Hamlet*, *The Town*, and *The Mansion* feature the Snopes family, which took over the town of Jefferson as old families like the Compsons disappeared. Many readers believe that Faulkner stopped writing great novels in the late 1930s. His later books—less pessimistic, more humorous—are also seen as less creative and profound. *The Sound and the Fury* may or may not be Faulkner's best novel—readers disagree about this. But almost all readers say it is his first great novel.

THE NOVEL

The Plot

In one sense, *The Sound and the Fury* takes place during Easter weekend, 1928. A carnival comes to Jefferson, Mississippi, where the Compson family lives. Mrs. Compson, a selfish, complaining woman, lies in bed all day while the black housekeeper, Dilsey, cooks and cleans. Mrs. Compson is a widow with two sons. Jason, who works in a hardware store, supports the family. The younger son, Benjamin, usually called Benjy, is an idiot. At thirty-three, he still has the mind of a child. Benjy is looked after by Luster, Dilsey's teenaged grandson. The household has one other member—Quentin, the seventeen-year-old daughter of Jason's older sister Candace, nicknamed Caddy. Caddy's husband left her when he realized that the infant she had just given birth to couldn't possibly be his. So Caddy sent the baby home for her mother and Dilsey to raise. Quentin is named for the Compson family's oldest son, who killed himself eighteen years earlier while he was a student at Harvard.

Not much occurs from Good Friday to Easter Sunday. The most important event is that a show comes to town. Luster takes Benjy to the golf course to look for lost quarters so that he can buy a ticket. Jason has extra tickets but burns them in the stove in front of Luster rather than give them to him. Jason is constantly criticizing Quentin. On Saturday night, Quentin slides down the drainpipe and runs away with a man from the show. Before she leaves, she steals Jason's savings. When Jason realizes on Sunday that both his niece and his money are gone, he chases futilely after them. What makes Jason angriest of all is that he can't tell anyone, not even the police, how much money Quentin actually took. The $3000 that Jason does report was his life's savings. But he'd also had $4000 that he'd stolen from Quentin. All along, when Caddy had sent money for Quentin's support, Jason had pretended that his mother tore up the checks, whereas, in reality, he had only given her forged ones to destroy. Secretly, he had cashed the real checks and hidden the money in his room, where Quentin found it. Since he wasn't supposed to have this $4000, he couldn't let on that it was gone. On his return home, Jason runs into Luster and Benjy. Luster has taken Benjy for a carriage ride but is driving around the square the wrong way. That makes Benjy uncomfortable and he is screaming. Jason turns the surrey around so it travels in the direction Benjy is used to.

That isn't much of a story. But *The Sound and the Fury* is about much more than that weekend in 1928. The Compsons' present is totally shaped by the past. Faulkner brings the past into the novel both through its structure—separate sections for each of the three Compson brothers, and one for the author—and through his style. Quentin's section is set entirely in the past. It takes place on the day before his suicide, June 2, 1910. As he prepares to die Quentin broods over what has gone on in his family. And although Benjy's section is set in the novel's present, 1928, the past is just like the present for Benjy. He can't tell the difference between the fire in the kitchen in 1928 and the fire in his mother's bedroom in 1900 when he was five. Benjy's section is filled with glimpses of the Compson children while growing up. Jason is able to cope with the present better than the other Compsons, but his section, too, contains many old resentments against his sister that he transfers to his niece.

Benjy's and Quentin's sections reveal the past as a backdrop against which the events of the present take place. The children's grandmother, whom they called Damuddy, died in 1898. In 1900, when Benjy was five, the family realized how severely retarded he was. He had originally been named Maury, for Mrs. Compson's brother. Now, because his mental retardation might reflect on the Bascombs, she wanted to change his name. Caddy's growing interest in boys in 1906–1908 upset both Quentin and Benjy, who in their different ways depended on her love. In 1909, Caddy slept with her boyfriend, Dalton Ames. Later she became pregnant and was forced to marry Herbert Head, a man she didn't love. At Caddy's wedding in April 1910, Benjy got drunk on champagne. After she left home, Benjy, waiting by the gate, ran after and grabbed a neighborhood girl who was walking home from school. Probably he confused her with Caddy, whom he used to wait for. In any case, in order to keep him from sexually attacking girls, the family had him castrated. Quentin dealt with his own distress about Caddy in a different way—a month later, he killed himself. Two years later, Mr. Compson, the children's father, died.

The brief summary of events on page 11 may be useful to you as you read the novel's first two sec-

Important events in *The Sound and the Fury*

The following list will help you understand the order of events in the story.

Damuddy's death—1898

Benjy's name change—1900

Christmas/Benjy and Caddy bring letter to Mrs. Patterson—sometime between 1900 and 1904

Caddy reaches puberty—1905–1909
>   Caddy uses perfume—about 1905
>   Benjy must sleep alone—1908
>   Quentin kisses Natalie—unknown, probably around 1906 or 1907
>   Caddy kisses a boy (the swing)—sometime between 1906 and 1909
>   Caddy has sex with Dalton Ames, Quentin fights with Dalton Ames—late summer 1909

Caddy's wedding—April 24, 1910
>   Wedding announcement
>   Quentin meets Herbert—April 22
>   Wedding eve—April 23

Benjy's castration—May or June 1910

Quentin's suicide—June 2, 1910

Breakup of Caddy's marriage/Mr. Compson brings baby Quentin back to Jefferson—1911

Mr. Compson's death—1912

Roskus's death—unknown, but after 1912

The present—1928
>   Benjy's 33rd birthday/the show/the girl Quentin runs away—April 7
>   Easter Sunday/theft discovered/Luster drives around monument—April 8

Death of Mrs. Compson/Jason fires Dilsey/Benjy institutionalized—1933

Librarian finds photograph of Caddy—1943

tions. But they aren't the whole story either. In an appendix that Faulkner wrote about fifteen years after *The Sound and the Fury* was published, he filled in more of the Compson's past and also brought their story forward to the 1940s. His history of the Compson family begins with the Indian chief who originally owned the land that became the town of Jefferson. The Appendix also reveals that, after Mrs. Compson died in 1933, Jason sold the family home and put Benjy in a state asylum. The old Compson place was turned into a boardinghouse and later was sold to a real estate developer. Caddy, according to the Appendix, married and divorced a Hollywood executive. In the 1940s the town librarian found a picture of a woman like Caddy with a Nazi general.

The Appendix links the novel to larger events in the country and the world. It also lets you see the story of the Compson family as a part of the history of the South. That history starts with the Indians and goes on through the era of slavery and the Civil War. Eventually the great old families like the Compsons die out. They are replaced by people Faulkner in other novels called the Snopeses— characters who share Jason's meanness and money-grubbing nature. The tract houses that eventually cover the Compson land are a symbol of what becomes of the South.

The Characters

MAJOR CHARACTERS

Jason Compson III

Jason Compson III is the father of Quentin, Caddy, Jason, and Benjy. The grandson of a governor and the son of a general, Compson is not living up to the family's distinguished past. All day he sits in a dusty law office, drinking whiskey, reading Latin, and writing nasty poems about the townspeople of Jefferson. But Compson is kind to the children. He is closest to Quentin and talks to him the most. The words "Father said" appear frequently in Quentin's recollections. But what he says to his son doesn't help Quentin very much. The day before he kills himself, Quentin remembers his father telling him that life is meaningless.

Is Mr. Compson a good father? Because he feels so defeated by life, he cannot draw close to his children or help them with their problems. He can send Quentin to Harvard and pay for Caddy's wedding, but he can't give his children real love and understanding.

Caroline Bascomb Compson

Like Faulkner's mother, Caroline Compson is never allowed to forget that her family wasn't as good as her husband's. But the resemblance ends there. Faulkner's mother was strong and energetic. Mrs. Compson is lazy and self-pitying. Time and again, you see her exaggerating minor problems and feeling sorry for herself. She shifts her responsibilities onto the black housekeeper Dilsey and then complains that Dilsey doesn't do things quickly enough.

Mrs. Compson cares more for appearances than for reality. She is furious when Caddy begins to become involved with boys, because it doesn't appear right. Later, when Caddy's daughter Quentin cuts school, Mrs. Compson worries that the principal will think she can't control her granddaughter. (It doesn't bother her that she really can't!) She has no real feeling for her children. She yells at

THE COMPSON FAMILY

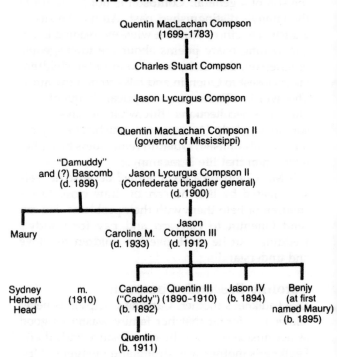

Quentin MacLachan Compson
(1699–1783)

Charles Stuart Compson

Jason Lycurgus Compson

Quentin MacLachan Compson II
(governor of Mississippi)

"Damuddy"
and (?) Bascomb
(d. 1898)

Jason Lycurgus Compson II
(Confederate brigadier general)
(d. 1900)

Maury

Caroline M.
(d. 1933)

Jason
Compson III
(d. 1912)

Sydney
Herbert
Head

m.
(1910)

Candace
("Caddy")
(b. 1892)

Quentin III
(1890–1910)

Jason IV
(b. 1894)

Benjy
(at first
named Maury)
(b. 1895)

Quentin
(b. 1911)

Versh, Dilsey's son, for taking Benjy out into the cold without dressing him warmly. She is afraid that Benjy will get sick, she says. But what really distresses her is that Benjy's sickness would create problems when she entertained Christmas guests.

Quentin Compson III

Named for his great-grandfather, the governor, Quentin is the brightest of the Compson children. Sending him to Harvard is his mother's dream. But

Quentin is too troubled to fulfill his parents' hopes. At the end of his first year at Harvard, he drowns himself.

Sex and love are the sources of Quentin's problems. He is frightened and disgusted by sex, and yearns for the time when he and his sister Caddy were children. He is obsessed with Caddy in two ways. He overemphasizes her virginity, which he equates with family honor. He feels that if Caddy is dishonored, the whole family will be destroyed. Quentin, therefore, is horribly upset when Caddy begins to sleep with boys. He hates the man she eventually marries. But at the same time that Quentin wants Caddy to remain a virgin, he has incestuous feelings toward her. He also imagines a mutual death pack for the two of them.

The past weighs heavily on Quentin. Present occurrences typically remind him of the past. He tries hard to understand what has happened to his family, and to find a meaning for life. But in the end, he cannot. Mr. Compson, unable to cope with the world, withdrew to his books and his bourbon. Quentin also withdraws, but his withdrawal—death—is much more extreme.

Readers react very differently to Quentin. Some sympathize with him. With a cold mother and a cynical father, they say, Quentin must have turned to his sister as the only source of love in the family. He then crumbled when she became less involved with him. Other readers, though, find Quentin as cold and self-involved as his parents. They say that he doesn't love Caddy, or Benjy—that he isn't capable of loving anyone. As you get deeper into the book, you will be able to make your own judgment.

Many readers find Quentin the least successful character in the book, because his concerns—honor, truth, virginity—seem so abstract. The fuss Quentin makes about Caddy's virginity is especially difficult to understand today. Even thirty and forty years ago, readers found it rather unbelievable that a young man would become so upset when his sister lost her virginity. Is Quentin just trying to find a way to live morally in a corrupt world, or is he a bit crazy? Is he a sensitive hero, or is he too weak and passive to be admired? At some point in your reading, you should come to grips with these questions.

Candace Compson (Caddy)

Faulkner once told an interviewer that *The Sound and the Fury* is "a tragedy of two lost women: Caddy and her daughter." He called Caddy "the beautiful one," "my heart's darling."

Faulkner was not the only one who loved Caddy. She was like a mother to her brothers. She sympathized with and encouraged Quentin. She took care of Benjy and explained his needs to others. Benjy describes her the way an infant might talk about its mother, if it could speak. He lets you know all the things she does to make him comfortable and happy. "Caddy smelled like trees," he often thinks.

Caddy is central to *The Sound and the Fury* in every way. She is the one active figure, climbing a tree, in Faulkner's image of the four children playing in the stream that inspired the novel. And her muddy underpants, in that image, symbolize her later promiscuity. As two of her brothers see it, Caddy's sexual looseness disgraced the Compson family. Her disappearance was a loss that her other brother, Benjy, continued to mourn seventeen years later. She drove Quentin to suicide and Jason to bitterness. And she ruined her daughter's life by leaving her with uncaring people.

Was Caddy really as bad as all that? Readers usually find her sympathetic. And many readers, especially women, may wonder whether Caddy actually did anything so awful. Social codes have changed since the 1950s, and women are no longer disgraced when they do what has always been acceptable for men to do. Today, a girl like Caddy might look to sex with boys for the love she can't get from her parents, but now she wouldn't be made to suffer so much for it. If she became pregnant, she would have other choices than tricking a man into marrying her, and then giving up her baby.

In *The Sound and the Fury* you never see Caddy directly, only as she is seen by her brothers. Why is this so, when Faulkner claimed that the image of her in the tree was the beginning of the novel? When a student asked him, Faulkner explained that "Caddy was still to me too beautiful and too moving to reduce her to telling what was going on . . . it would be more passionate to see her through somebody else's eyes, I thought." Some readers point out that Faulkner—even more than other American novelists of his generation—was not very good at creating female characters. Most of the women in Faulkner's other novels were either sexual and not very bright or sexless.

Jason Compson IV

The Appendix calls Jason Compson IV the "first sane Compson" since the original Quentin Compson left Scotland for America. Certainly Jason seems more "normal" than either of his brothers. But that doesn't make Jason a sympathetic character. His values are the common ones of his society—making money and getting ahead. Unlike Quentin, who is lost in the past, Jason has no respect for the past at all. He makes fun of his famous ancestors, and he sells the family home as soon as his mother dies.

The section of the novel that Jason narrates is much easier to read than Benjy's or Quentin's. Events in the present do not send him into the past as consistently as they do his brothers. Whereas Benjy's language is simple and poetic and Quentin's is rhetorical and romantic, Jason's language is coarse. Jason blames other people for his troubles. We can see, though, that he brings many of them on himself. Jason also usually has something nasty to say about others.

Jason's section is largely taken up with his battle with his niece Quentin. Quentin eventually defeats him by running away and taking all his money with her. But we see Jason throughout the novel, as Quentin and especially Benjy think of the scenes of their childhood. Even as a boy, Jason was mean, spiteful, and a liar. Yet he is the only one of the Compson children who is able to function in the modern world with any degree of success. What does that say about Faulkner's opinion of his society?

Benjamin Compson
The Compsons named their third child Maury, after Mrs. Compson's ne'er-do-well brother. But when they realized something was wrong with him, they decided to change his name. Quentin suggested

the biblical name Benjamin, which is usually short-
ened to Benjy or Ben.

In the novel's present time, April 1928, Benjy is
celebrating his thirty-third birthday. He still has the
mind of a child, however, and does not understand
the connection between cause and effect. For example, he thinks, "The hand went away," not realizing that a person withdrew it. There is no evidence that Benjy can talk, since neither he nor any
other character ever reports a word he says. What
we know of Benjy comes mostly from his thoughts.
He loves bright things, firelight and mirrors. He
also loves the smell of rain (which reminds him of
Quentin and of his father) and the smell of trees
(which reminds him of Caddy). He likes things to
be in familiar order, as you see at the end of the
novel when Luster drives him the wrong way around
the town square. Caddy is what he loves best, and
he loses her. In fact, the overpowering feeling of
Benjy's section of the novel is loss.

People's reactions to him reveal a great deal about
what they are really like. Caddy understands him
perfectly, and he loves her best. Mrs. Compson,
although she talks about "my poor baby," doesn't
observe what he needs. Dilsey, the black housekeeper, is also good to Benjy, as are her sons Versh
and T.P. (Her grandson, Luster, likes to tease him.)
To a lesser extent, Benjy likes his father and Quentin. But Jason is mean to Benjy and constantly makes
fun of him. So does Caddy's daughter, Quentin.
Benjy has an instinctive sense of what's happening. He knows when Caddy's been with a boy, for
example; and the other children say that he can
smell Damuddy's death.

Only in the book's final section do you get a

description of Benjy. There the narrator tells you that he is a big man with fine pale hair and corn-flower blue eyes. He walks "with a shambling gait, like a trained bear," and he drools. In the course of the other sections, you learn various facts about Benjy's life. Shortly after Caddy's wedding, he chases after a little girl in the street. His parents, fearing that Benjy has developed sexual urges, have him castrated. You also learn that in 1933, Jason commits him to the state asylum in Jackson. You can imagine what kind of life he will have there.

Readers have various reactions to Benjy. Some readers have identified Benjy with Christ, pointing out that in the novel he is thirty-three, the age of Christ at his death. The action in the book takes place during the days between Good Friday, the day of the Crucifixion, and Easter Sunday. And in order to quiet Benjy at the novel's end, Luster gives him a narcissus, a traditional symbol of Christ. Is Benjy a Christ figure, and is his suffering meant to redeem the members of his family or human-kind? Or is he a failed Christ, appropriate for a modern, meaningless world? It's hard to say. An-other reader has advanced a psychological inter-pretation based on theories of Sigmund Freud. He thinks that Jason represents the ego, Quentin the superego, and Benjy the id—the most fundamen-tal level of the personality, according to Freudians.

Dilsey Gibson

Dilsey, the Compson's black housekeeper, is working in the kitchen when the clock, which is not adjusted correctly, strikes five times. "Eight o'clock," Dilsey thinks to herself, automatically correcting the hour. That is a reflection of Dilsey's most important characteristic. Of all the people in the Compson household, Dilsey is the only one certain about the boundaries between past and present. She is also the only one who can live in the real world without abandoning her values. Dilsey keeps the family going from day to day. Of course, she is not really a Compson, although she tells her sons that they are part of the family.

Dilsey, like Caddy, is an enormous source of warmth in the novel. Caddy, however, was destroyed by her sexuality while Dilsey is seen as asexual, and her warmth is safely maternal. She takes good care of the Compson children, and her generous heart goes out to the two most vulnerable. She knows what pleases Benjy. She protects the girl Quentin, keeping Jason from beating her. Dilsey knows how to work around the whiny Mrs. Compson, flattering her but not doing everything she wants.

In addition, Dilsey has a life of her own. She is a good mother to her three children and encourages them to work hard and behave properly. At the same time, she teaches them how to survive in a world run by whites. She loves the good people around her. "De good Lawd dont keer whether he smart or not," she tells her daughter Frony when Frony wonders whether they should bring Benjy to their church. On Easter Sunday, Dilsey is deeply moved by a black preacher's powerful sermon. Christ's Resurrection is alive for Dilsey as for no other character in the book.

Faulkner's comment on Dilsey in the Appendix consists of two words: "They endured." And indeed, the Compson's black servants survived the family's ruin. Dilsey becomes a sort of commentator on the entire novel when she says, after the Easter service, "I seed de beginnin, en now I sees de endin." To some extent, Dilsey shares some of the family's original values. She fights against Jason's betrayal of those values for as long as she can.

Some readers view Dilsey as the most heroic figure in *The Sound and the Fury*. They see Dilsey's endurance as strength. Others point out that the endurance is only passive. Dilsey can't affect events. She can only comfort their innocent victims. In deciding what you think of Dilsey, you'll want to pay close attention to the Easter service. It is a good guide to what she believes.

Quentin (Caddy's daughter)

You don't really know much about Caddy's daughter Quentin. Caddy sends the girl home to Jefferson after her divorce from Herbert Head. Jason steals the checks Caddy sends for Quentin's support, and won't let Caddy see the girl when she comes to town.

Quentin is a hard, angry girl. She wears too much makeup, cuts school, and becomes involved with men. Jason continually picks on her, but she gives back as good as she gets. Quentin blames Jason for her behavior. She's bad, she says, but Jason made her that way. Do you agree?

Quentin eventually runs off with a man who came to Jefferson with a traveling show. Before she leaves, she takes all Jason's money—both his savings and the money Caddy had meant for her. It is difficult to predict what will become of Quentin, and Faulkner's Appendix doesn't help. She is not likely to have a very happy life, however.

In some ways, Quentin's story turns out to be something like Caddy's. She turns to men to escape from her family. But where Caddy was loving and warm, Quentin is cold and bitter. She is mean to Dilsey, the only person who treats her with any affection. Quentin often says that she wishes she had never been born.

Versh, T.P., Frony

Versh, T.P., and Frony are Dilsey's children. The boys, Versh and T.P., look after Benjy in the early portions of the book. Frony helps out in the kitchen. In the Appendix, Faulkner pictures T.P. as grown, a sharp dude in cheap clothes on Beale Street in Memphis. The Appendix also tells you that Frony married a Pullman porter and made a home for Dilsey in Memphis after Mrs. Compson died.

Luster

Luster, Frony's son, is probably about seventeen in 1928, although the Appendix says that he is fourteen. Luster's job is to look after Benjy. He's not as good at it as his uncles were, and he likes to tease Benjy more. As the book ends, he drives Benjy the wrong way around the town square.

Roskus Gibson

Roskus, Dilsey's husband, also works for the Compsons. He dies some time after Mr. Compson.

MINOR CHARACTERS

Dalton Ames

Dalton is the first man Caddy sleeps with. Quentin fights him in an attempt to avenge what he considers the family honor, but Dalton wins easily.

Herbert Head

A banker from Indianapolis, Head marries Caddy Compson. When he realizes that she was pregnant by another man at the time of their wedding, he leaves her. Jason Compson never gets the job that Herbert promised him at his bank.

Earl and Uncle Job

Earl is the owner of the hardware store where Jason works. Uncle Job is an old black who works there too. You see both of these men through their interactions with Jason. Jason continually starts fights with Earl and often picks on Uncle Job. Uncle Job takes care of himself, however.

Maury Bascomb

Maury Bascomb, Mrs. Compson's no-good brother, is always borrowing money from her. Benjy was originally named for him. Once, several days before Christmas, Uncle Maury uses the Compson children to deliver a note to his mistress, Mrs. Patterson.

Lorraine

Lorraine is Jason Compson's mistress in Memphis. The only way that Jason can relate to a woman is by paying her.

Deacon

Deacon is an old black who does errands for Harvard students. Quentin gives him his suicide notes. Quentin's relationship with Deacon shows that he misses the South.

Shreve MacKenzie

Shreve, a Canadian, is Quentin's roommate at Harvard. The Appendix tells us that Shreve eventually became a surgeon and returned to Canada. He also is a character in Faulkner's later novel *Absalom, Absalom!*

Gerald Bland and Mrs. Bland

Gerald Bland is a Harvard student whose attitude toward women reminds Quentin of Dalton Ames. Mrs. Bland is proud of her son's success with women.

Julio

Julio is the brother of the little Italian girl who follows Quentin around on his last day in Cambridge. The presence of Julio in the novel shows that other brothers care about their sisters.

Other Elements

SETTING

Most of *The Sound and the Fury* takes place in and around the Compson family home in Jefferson, Mississippi. This was the second novel that Faulkner set in Jefferson. (*Sartoris*, 1929, was the first.) As the years went on, he continued to tell stories about the town and the surrounding countryside. He gave it the Indian name Yoknapatawpha County to emphasize that the area was settled by Indians. Yoknapatawpha was based on Lafayette County, Mississippi, whose capital was Oxford (where Faulker spent most of his life).

In creating Yoknapatawpha County, Faulkner did more than describe a landscape. He also populated it with people, most of whom knew or had some connection with each other. Several times a minor character in a novel appeared as a major character in a later novel. For example, Quentin Compson is the conarrator of *Absalom, Absalom!*, which was published six years after *The Sound and the Fury*. For *Absalom, Absalom!* Faulkner drew a map of Yoknapatawpha County, showing where characters in his various novels lived and where events took place. He signed the map "William Faulkner, Sole Owner and Proprietor," making the point that the county was his invention. Because so many of his novels are set in the same place and so many of the characters appear more than once, it almost seems as if Faulkner wrote only one enormous novel.

In *The Sound and the Fury*, you see something of what Jefferson looks like. Because the novel is mainly concerned with the minds of the characters, however, physical setting is not important.

Faulkner once told an interviewer that he had discovered that "my own little postage stamp of native soil was worth writing about and that I would never live long enough to exhaust it. . . ." Some readers believe that his focus on Yoknapatawpha showed he was only concerned with Southern themes. Others say Faulkner's frequent use of Yoknapatawpha and its people lent it an almost mythical status. There he could explore the universal issues of human life. Either way, few American writers have returned to the same setting as often as Faulkner.

THEMES

William Faulkner gives you two hints about the major themes of *The Sound and the Fury*. One is its title, which is taken from William Shakespeare's play *Macbeth.* In Act V, as he is about to be defeated and killed, Macbeth hears that his wife is dead. He responds:

> Tomorrow, and tomorrow, and tomorrow,
> Creeps in this petty pace from day to day
> To the last syllable of recorded time;
> And all our yesterdays have lighted fools
> The way to dusty death. Out, out, brief candle!
> Life's but a walking shadow, a poor player
> That struts and frets his hour upon the stage
> And then is heard no more; it is a tale
> Told by an idiot, full of sound and fury,
> Signifying nothing.

Like Macbeth's view of life, *The Sound and the Fury* is a tale told (in part) by an idiot, Benjy Compson. Macbeth believed that life was without meaning, and that time brought only defeat. Some readers say Faulkner felt the same way, while others disagree.

The second hint about the themes of *The Sound and the Fury* is Faulkner's frequent claim that the novel was an attempt to tell the story of a little girl with muddy drawers who was watching her grandmother's funeral from a tree while her brothers waited below. This alerts you to the novel's stress on point of view and to the importance of the relationship between the Compson children as it changes over time.

1. THE PASSING OF TIME

As you can tell from the frequent mention of watches and clocks in *The Sound and the Fury*, its characters are as concerned about the passage of time as Macbeth. Each of them has a special relationship to time.

Benjy, whose section opens the book, lives outside of time. For him, the past is as real as the present. In 1928 he stands at the gate, still expecting Caddy, who left home in 1910. Time does not exist for Benjy because he lives only in his senses.

Quentin, for his part, wants to step out of time. His section contains many references to time and timepieces. Quentin imagines himself and Caddy burning together in a pure timeless flame. But the only way he can remove himself from time is to kill himself. For Quentin, like Benjy, the past constantly intrudes in the present. Quentin cannot leave the past because he is obsessed by his problems and memories.

Time is also important to Jason. He is always finding out what time it is, always hurrying to do something or yelling at other people for being late. Jason is constantly measuring time, the same way he's always counting his money. Jason lives only in the present, without a past.

Dilsey, however, is aware of both past and present. When she hears the clock (which is not set correctly) in the Compson house strike five, she knows that it is eight o'clock. Of all the characters in the novel, only she knows what time it really is. She can both respect the values of the past and function in the present.

2. THE FALL OF A FAMILY

The Compsons are a family on the decline. Quentin Compson II governed the state, and Jason II was a general (although not especially successful). But Jason III is drinking his life away. And his children are even worse. One commits suicide, another disgraces herself, the third is a thief, and the fourth is an idiot. The only grandchild is bitter and angry, with little likelihood of leading a productive life.

What has gone wrong with the Compson family? Some readers point to the lack of love. Mrs. Compson is self-absorbed and doesn't care about her children. Mr. Compson is not able to express his feeling for them. He fills his son Quentin's head with cynical, life-denying ideas. These readers say that Quentin, Caddy, and Jason—and later the girl Quentin—all react—in different ways—to the lack of parental love.

3. THE FALL OF THE SOUTH

Some readers say the fall of the Compsons is not only the story of an individual family. They see it as a story about the South as a region. For these readers, the major explanation for the fate of the Compsons is found in the society of which they're part, not in the psychology of the family members.

You can find evidence for this approach in the Appendix. The Appendix was written more than fifteen years after *The Sound and the Fury* was published and may represent Faulkner's rethinking of the book. During the intervening years, he had written several novels. Two in particular—*Absalom, Absalom!* and *Go Down, Moses*—deal with the history of the South. In the Appendix, Faulkner may have added his interpretation of Southern history to the Compson family saga. In *Absalom, Absalom!* and *Go Down, Moses*, Faulkner pictures taking land from Indians and enslaving blacks as twin curses on white Southerners. Slavery is not examined in the Appendix to *The Sound and the Fury*. However, when a student once asked Faulkner, "What is the trouble with the Compsons?" the novelist answered, "They are still living in the attitudes of 1859 or '60"—that is, before the Civil War.

The only Compson who can cope with the twentieth century is Jason. He allows first a boarding house and then a housing development to be built on the old family land. Such enterprises are typical of the modern South, and Faulkner hated them. He told another student that "there are too many Jasons in the South who can be successful, just as there are too many Quentins in the South who are too sensitive to face its reality."

Thus, there is some evidence that the decline of the Compson family parallels the decline of the old South. You'll have to decide whether evidence for this interpretation is limited to the Appendix. Is this theme an afterthought, or an integral part of the novel?

4. THE MODERN WORLD

Faulkner doesn't have much good to say about the modern world. Jason, the character most fully a part of it, is the least appealing character for most readers. Jason is not the only Compson child who adopts modern values that repel most readers. Caddy marries a Hollywood executive, divorces him, and seems to wind up, in the 1940s, with a Nazi general. The girl Quentin, too, is spiritually empty.

Some readers suggest that the fate of Quentin and of Benjy indicates the impossibility of living in the commercial world with either idealism (like Quentin) or innocence (like Benjy).

The bleakness of the novel's present (and the projection of the future in the Appendix) contrasts sharply with the view of the past. The past appears either as calm and serene (as in Quentin's recollection, at the end of his section, of his grandfather) or as warm and secure (as in Benjy's memories of the family around the fireplace in 1900). All the Compson children, except Jason, long for the past.

The emptiness of modern life was a frequent topic for writers in the first decades of the twentieth century. Writers whom Faulkner knew in New Orleans and in Paris frequently dealt with this theme. T. S. Eliot's poem "The Waste Land," published seven years before *The Sound and the Fury*, is one example. Another is a collection of essays by Southern writers, called *I'll Take My Stand*, published only one year earlier. These writers rejected the values of modern urban civilization, as did Faulkner.

5. SHADOW AND SUBSTANCE

Macbeth calls life "a walking shadow," and *The Sound and the Fury* contains numerous references to shadows—one reader counted 53! Most of the shadows are in Quentin's section. Quentin is always seeing the shadows of things—curtains, bridges, trees, himself. He is unable to look straight at things. He feels the presence of the past like a shadow over his life and also feels like the shadow of his ancestors. Quentin never really accomplishes what he dreams about. In the end he is unable to sleep with Caddy, to cut her throat, or to shoot Dalton Ames. When T. S. Eliot wrote in his poem "The Hollow Men," "Between the motion/And the act. Falls the Shadow," he could have been talking about Quentin.

6. LEARNING THE TRUTH

Related to the theme of shadow and substance is the theme of how truth is discovered. *The Sound and the Fury* is a story told from four points of view. You find out what really happened as stories are told and retold.

Because the structure of *The Sound and the Fury* is so unusual and so difficult, figuring out what is going on absorbs the reader. It is impossible to understand the Benjy section until you have finished the entire novel. You become a detective, looking for clues, weighing one character's version against another's, filling in the gaps in people's stories.

7. THE MEANING OF LIFE

Does life have meaning? Or is it, as Macbeth says, "a tale/Told by an idiot, full of sound and fury,/Signifying nothing"?

Some characters in the novel feel life is meaningless. Mr. Compson is one such character. Quentin struggles to find meaning in life but eventually cannot and kills himself. For Jason, the only meaning in life is money.

Dilsey is the only character in the novel with a clear sense of purpose to life. She derives this in part from her religious convictions. Listening to a sermon on Christ's Resurrection, she is able to make sense out of the story of the Compsons. Her life also takes on meaning from her warm relationships with the people around her.

Benjy has no sense of life's meaning, because he cannot really think. But he has a feeling for order, and he is furious when—as at the novel's end—that order is violated.

As you read *The Sound and the Fury*, ask yourself whether the novel's message is that life is meaningless. Do you think that Faulkner identifies most with Quentin's yearning to escape into the past or with Dilsey's Christian faith? Or does he sympathize with both?

8. THE WAR BETWEEN GOOD AND EVIL

The war between good and evil—between integrity and irresponsibility—is a major theme in many of Faulkner's novels. In *The Sound and the Fury*, integrity is represented by innocent Benjy, idealistic Quentin, and good-hearted Dilsey. Irresponsibility rests with Mr. and Mrs. Compson, who don't care enough about their children; with hypocritical, alcoholic Uncle Maury Bascomb; with promiscuous Caddy (although her love for her brothers reveals the goodness in her); with angry and dishonest Jason; and with dishonest Quentin, Caddy's daughter. At the end of *The Sound and the Fury*, is good ahead, or does evil carry the day? There is evidence for both views.

STYLE

The style of *The Sound and the Fury* is extremely complicated. The book has four narrators, each of whom talks and thinks differently, as well as has different concerns. The fourth section of the book, narrated by the author, contains clear, descriptive writing. Although marked by long sentences and some unusual words ("Two tears slid down her fallen cheeks, in and out of the myriad coruscations of immolation and abnegation and time"), it is straightforward.

In the first three sections, however, Faulkner uses writing techniques that were just beginning to be used in the early decades of the twentieth century. These are stream-of-consciousness and interior monologue. Stream-of-consciousness is an attempt to reproduce the character's thought pattern. The writer tries to put the thoughts down on the page just as they would have passed through the character's mind. Because one thought may lead to a rather unrelated thought, stream-of-consciousness prose moves in an apparently random way from one subject to another. Usually the character "free associates"—one object reminds him or her of another.

Although Benjy's and Quentin's sections both employ stream-of-consciousness, they have very different styles. Benjy thinks in simple sentences and has a limited vocabulary. Quentin, on the other hand, thinks either in extremely long sentences or in sentence fragments. He likes words that refer to abstract ideas, and he piles adjectives one atop another. Where Benjy's memory rarely returns to the same story twice (sometimes he finishes a story, sometimes not), Quentin comes back again and again. Quentin also repeats names and phrases.

The book as a whole is rich in imagery and symbolism, which are used to the fullest in Quentin's section. He frequently refers to water, shadows, watches, sisters, and the smell of honeysuckle, which reminds him of sex. Faulkner uses italics to mark time shifts within Benjy's and Quentin's sections. However, some time shifts are not italicized. Faulkner felt the book should be printed in different-colored inks to make it easier for the reader.

Jason's section is stylistically different from Benjy's or Quentin's. It is an interior monologue, consisting entirely of his thoughts. But these thoughts are presented rationally, not in the poetic free association of stream-of-consciousness. Jason's monologue sounds like something a person would say. Jason thinks in short, hurried sentences. His language is often vulgar, slangy, and sarcastic.

Faulkner accurately reproduces the speech of the black characters. For instance, you can watch as the black minister switches from educated black speech to a more folksy language in the course of a sermon.

POINT OF VIEW

The Sound and the Fury is told from four points of view. Each of the first three sections is narrated in the first person by a Compson brother, and the fourth section is narrated in the third person by the author.

All of the Compson brothers are limited as narrators in some way. You shouldn't completely trust any of their versions of events.

Because he is mentally retarded, Benjy can't interpret what's happening. He tells you what things smelled like, and whether they made him cry, but he can't tell you why things happened or what someone else was feeling. However, he does remember conversations. Sometimes you can figure things out that Benjy himself can't; for example, you can see that the children in the "Damuddy's funeral" scene have the same personality traits they will have as adults.

Although Quentin is very intelligent, he also has limitations as a narrator. He is so obsessed by Caddy's loss of virginity and by his father's philosophy that he can think of little else. Quentin remembers some incidents that you recognize from the Benjy section, but most of what he focuses on is new. Still, because of his compulsive interest in time, shadows, and sisters, Quentin doesn't notice much about other people or about what is going on around him.

Jason, too, is a limited narrator, because he sees things only from his own point of view. Jason, as he sees it, is always right, and the world is always wrong. Like his brother Quentin, he isn't very good at observing other people. But Jason does report conversations, and they tell you a lot about what other people think of Jason.

The fourth narrator generally describes events objectively. He makes some judgments, however. The narrator expresses great sympathy for Benjy, likening his wailing to "all time and injustice and sorrow become vocal for an instant." The narrator, on the other hand, has little sympathy for Quentin. The description of her room after she has left is downright nasty.

FORM AND STRUCTURE

The Sound and the Fury is divided into four sections. The first and third are approximately equal in length. The second is about thirty pages longer, and the fourth, about thirty pages shorter. Each section is distinctly marked by a date on its first page; three sections are dated in the novel's present and one in the past. Each section is marked by a change of narrator.

The narration does not move chronologically—that is, it does not begin at the beginning and proceed toward the end. But you can't say that it is told in flashbacks, because that implies you are standing firmly in the present and looking back at the past. In *The Sound and the Fury*, the present and past are so mixed together that the reader often can't tell the difference between them any better than the characters.

Because the first section, Benjy's, concentrates on what happened when the Compson children were young, the story almost does begin at the beginning. (The Appendix, which Faulkner suggested be placed at the beginning of the book, begins the story with the Indian chief who sold the first Compson the land and carries the story beyond the end of the novel proper.)

Some readers object to the order of the sections. In particular, they wonder why Faulkner put the Benjy section first, because it is difficult and cannot be fully understood until you have finished the novel. Some readers suggest that the Jason or Dilsey sections, both of which are easier to understand, should have preceded Benjy's.

However, there are reasons for the order Faulkner chose. One follows from the book's title. Macbeth called life "a tale/Told by an idiot, full of sound and fury,/Signifying nothing." It makes sense, therefore, to open *The Sound and the Fury* with a tale told by an idiot. More important is that, as noted just before, Benjy's childhood memories form the chronological beginnings of the novel proper. Quentin continues the story in the years just before 1910 and focuses on the events of that year. Jason's main interest begins in 1911, the year he didn't get the job in Herbert's bank and Caddy sent baby Quentin home. Jason and the narrator in the fourth section concentrate on 1928.

Faulkner the storyteller may have had some tricks up his sleeve in starting with the Benjy section. When you read the Quentin section, you understand some things that were unclear in Benjy's. When you read the Jason and fourth sections, you understand even more. So Faulkner starts you out with something that is hard to make sense of, and then gives you more and more clues so that in the end you have the information to understand the first part. *The Sound and the Fury* is a novel you should not only read, but *reread*.

The Story

APRIL SEVENTH, 1928
(BENJY'S SECTION)

You are about to read a section that is probably unlike anything you've ever read, for the narrator of these pages, Benjamin Compson, is severely retarded. How does such a person think? No one really knows for sure. William Faulkner created in Benjy a character who feels things deeply. Benjy can't interpret what is going on and doesn't understand the connection between cause and effect. But in simple sentences, most concerned with how things look, smell, and feel, Benjy manages to tell you a lot.

Benjy's section is set, as its title indicates, in the novel's present. April 7, 1928, is the Saturday before Easter Sunday. It is also Benjy's thirty-third birthday. Benjy is cared for by Luster, the son of Dilsey's daughter Frony. As he goes about his day, first outdoors with Luster and later in the house, events in the present trigger Benjy's mind to focus on events of the past. Benjy, however, can't distinguish between past events and present events. The earlier events are as current to him as anything actually happening in the present.

At first it may be hard to follow the narration in these pages. For example, Benjy first tells you that "I could see them hitting. They were coming toward where the flag was." What could this possibly mean? It turns out that Benjy is watching men play golf. The first paragraph of his section is a good description of what a game of golf would

look like if you didn't understand it. It might help
to form a mental picture of Benjy's words rather
than just react to their strangeness.

Although, on first reading, the section may con-
fuse you, it *is* possible to follow. Every word refers
to a specific event. To help you to figure out what
is going on and to follow the changes in time between the present and various moments in the past,
you will find a list of the events described in Benjy's
section in a Note at the end of this discussion.
Besides that list, there are a number of clues that
can help you follow the action at any given point
in this section. They are:

Type changes. A shift from roman to italic type, or
back the other way, often (but not always) signals
a movement in time. Where the time changes are
not marked by changes in type, you will have to
be alert to other elements.

Benjy's caretaker. When Benjy was a small boy, he
was taken care of by Versh, Dilsey and Roskus's
oldest son. The presence of Versh means that an
event occurred between 1898 and 1902. Versh was
succeeded by their second son, T.P. If T.P. is taking care of Benjy, the event took place in 1905 or
later. In the novel's present time, 1928, Luster, Dilsey's grandson, is looking after Benjy. Any reference to Luster as caretaker means that we are in
the present. (But be careful. In the scenes of Damuddy's death, which take place in 1900, T.P. is
present as a little boy, although Versh is the one
in charge of Benjy. At another time, when T.P. is
in charge of Benjy, Luster is a baby, playing with
baby Quentin. Remember: you are looking for
Benjy's caretaker.)

Patterns of description. Benjy's mind keeps returning to the same few events, and he usually describes them the same way. By paying attention to
recurring images, you can usually tell when a scene
is taking place. References to the branch (stream),
for example, or to Caddy's muddy drawers point
to Damuddy's death in 1898. Mentions of fire, rain,
or mirrors signal the changing of Benjy's name in
1900. References to the cold and to other characters
telling Benjy to keep his hands in his pockets evoke
the time when Uncle Maury sent Caddy and Benjy
to deliver a letter to Mrs. Patterson in approximately 1902. Mention of drinking "sasprilluh" refers to Caddy's wedding in 1910.

Three further warnings are in order. The first is
that the narrator of this section was named Maury
when he was born. His name was changed to Benjamin when he was five years old, in 1900. So in
the very earliest scenes, he is referred to as Maury,
not Benjy. For example, when Caddy tells Versh
to carry Maury up the hill, she is talking about the
character later known as Benjy. A second warning:
Read closely, and don't let your mind drift. If you
pay attention, you can follow the action. If you
don't, it will really seem like "a tale/Told by an
idiot." Finally, you will not understand the full
meaning of everything in this section until later in
the book. However, if you keep at it, the meanings
and events will all fall into place.

The page numbers used in The Story section refer to the Vintage Books paperback edition (New
York: Random House, 1954). The page number
marks the beginning of a scene. The first three
words have also been included to help identify the

scene for you, since several scenes may appear on one page.

NOTE: Events in Benjy's section   The following list places the events described in Benjy's section in chronological order. It begins with the earliest, when Benjy was three, and ends in the novel's present. However, this is not the order in which the events are presented in the section. Benjy's mind shifts back and forth, returning to each past event several times. These scenes are explained in greater detail following this Note.

The Distant Past

The children playing in the branch and Damuddy's death (1898)   In these scenes, the children are all very young. They frequently talk about the death of their grandmother. Dilsey's son Versh is taking care of Benjy. These scenes occur on pages 19, 22, 23, 25, 38, 39, 42, 44, 45, 53, 74, 76, 89, 90.

Benjy's name change (1900)   These scenes take place indoors. Benjy does not turn to them until the second half of the section, when Luster brings him into the house for his birthday cake. These scenes often contain images of Benjy looking into the fire or a mirror or listening to the rain. See pages 67, 69, 70, 74, 75, 76, 80, 82, 83, 84, 85, 86, 87.

The Patterson episode (sometime between 1900 and 1904) It is impossible to date these scenes precisely. Most of them occur just before Christmas, and there are frequent references to the cold and to the need for keeping hands inside pockets. These scenes can also be identified by references to Uncle Maury and to Mrs. or Mr. Patterson. See pages 3, 5, 13, 14, 51.

The Middle Past

Caddy reaches puberty (1905–1909)   In several scenes, Benjy remembers how Caddy began to get involved with boys and to move away from him. The main image here is that Caddy no longer smells like trees. T.P. is the attendant. These scenes include:

- Caddy uses perfume (around 1905), page 48.
- Benjy must sleep alone (1908), pages 51, 53.
- Caddy in the swing (sometime between 1906 and 1909), pp. 55, 56.
- Caddy loses her virginity (1909), pages 83, 84.

Caddy's wedding (April 1910)   T.P. is the attendant. The main images are the "sassprilluh" that T.P. and Benjy drink, Caddy in a white veil, and Caddy not smelling like trees. See pages 23, 43, 44, 45, 46.

Benjy's castration (May or June 1910)   The principal image is Benjy waiting at the gate for Caddy, page 62.

Three deaths (1910–?)   In these scenes, dogs howl, and Benjy and other characters cry and moan.

- Quentin's suicide (June 1910), page 33.
- Mr. Compson's death (1912), pages 32, 35, 37, 39.
- The trip to the cemetery (sometime after 1912), page 8.

• Roskus's death (date unknown), pages 38, 39.

The Present (April 1928)
These scenes can be identified by the presence of Luster and by references to the golf course and the show. See pages 1, 5, 8, 12, 14, 21, 23, 38, 42, 55, 56, 58, 64, 68, 69, 71, 79, 80, 81, 83, 85, 86, 87, 88, 89, 90.

Page 1: "Through the fence . . ." (1928)
Benjy and Luster are walking along the fence that separates the Compson property from the adjoining golf course. Whenever the golfers cry "Caddie!" Benjy begins to moan. As you will soon learn, Caddy is the name of his lost sister. Luster tells you that today is Benjy's thirty-third birthday. Later it will be celebrated with candles and a cake. Luster wants to find a quarter he lost in the grass so that he can go to the show that night. Failing that, he hopes to find a golf ball he can sell back to the players. As they duck under a fence onto the course, Benjy gets caught on a nail.

Page 3: *"Caddy uncaught me . . ."* (December 23, sometime between 1900 and 1905)
Getting caught in the fence in the present sends Benjy's mind back to a time in the past when he had gotten caught in the fence. Note that Faulkner has signaled the move back in time by changing into italics. (Sometimes we know the date of a scene because it occurred at about the same time as an event whose date we know [like Quentin's suicide]. Sometimes there is internal evidence—for example, the children may mention their ages. In

this scene, however, there is no definite indication of the date.) In this scene, Caddy and Benjy crawl under a fence. It is just before Christmas and very cold.

Page 3: " 'It's too cold . . .' " (December 23, sometime between 1900 and 1905)
Earlier in the same day as the preceding scene, Versh bundles Benjy up and takes him outdoors. They wait at the gate for Caddy to come home from school.

NOTE: Remember this scene. The image of waiting at the gate for Caddy will become important later in the story.

Versh keeps telling Benjy to keep his hands in his pockets. When Caddy arrives, she rubs his hands to warm them. To Benjy, Caddy smells like trees. Throughout the novel, this is the way he identifies her.

NOTE: Mrs. Compson Within the space of two pages, this scenes tells you a great deal about Mrs. Compson. She calls him Benjamin when everyone else calls him Benjy. When Benjy makes noise, Versh understands that he wants to go outdoors, but she doesn't—Versh is more observant of Benjy's needs than Mrs. Compson. Mrs. Compson says—not for the last time in the novel—that Benjy is "a judgment on me." She seems to care more about herself than about Benjy. Mrs. Compson pays no attention to Dilsey's needs, either. She proposes sending Benjy to the kitchen even though Dilsey is feverishly preparing for Christmas dinner.

In this scene, you meet Uncle Maury, Mrs. Compson's brother. He flatters her, saying she'll worry herself sick over Benjy. To help keep up her strength, he makes her a hot toddy. Uncle Maury is himself a big drinker, as you will later find out. He's also always sponging off the Compsons.

Page 5: "What are you . . ." (1928)
Benjy is probably moaning because he is thinking about Caddy. Luster doesn't understand this, but gives Benjy a flower to quiet him. This is your first indication of Benjy's great love of flowers.

Page 5: " 'What is it.' " (December 23, 19—)
This is a continuation of the scene before last, which was interrupted by Luster's reaction to Benjy's moaning. When Caddy returns from school, she and Versh bring Benjy indoors. Mrs. Compson hassles Caddy and Versh and calls Benjy her "poor baby." But as Caddy explains to him, he isn't a poor baby at all—he has her.

Page 8: "Can't you shut . . ." (1928)
Again, Luster complains as Benjy moans with feelings of Caddy's love. They notice the new wheel on the family carriage.

Page 8: " 'Git in, now . . .' " (1912 or 1913)
Seeing the wheel on the carriage in 1928 sends Benjy into the past, when Dilsey drew attention to the dilapidated wheel on the surrey. This is typical of the first section of the novel: As Luster and Benjy

move about the Compson property, Benjy thinks about events that took place at various locations.

In this scene, T.P. drives the surrey to the cemetery so that Mrs. Compson and Benjy can visit Quentin's and Mr. Compson's graves. You later learn that Quentin died in 1910 and Mr. Compson two years after. So this scene occurs either shortly after Mr. Compson's death in 1912 or a year or two following. Luster is a baby, and so is Caddy's daughter Quentin. Quentin was born in 1911, but you don't know exactly how old she is here.

Dilsey calms Benjy by giving him a flower. Mrs. Compson, as you have come to expect, criticizes Dilsey and T.P., and calls Benjy a "judgment." They stop at the hardware store where Jason works. He calls Benjy a "damn loony," which tells you something about Jason. He also speaks harshly to his mother. You probably are not surprised when Jason reveals that Uncle Maury is borrowing money from Mrs. Compson.

Page 12: *"Cry baby, Luster . . ."* **(1928)**
Again in the present, Luster complains about Benjy's moaning. They walk by the barn.

Page 13: **" 'Keep your hands . . .' "**
(December 23, 19—)
In a continuation of the December 23 scene, Caddy and Benjy walk by the barn. Caddy warns Benjy to keep his hands in his pockets because it is so cold. The two children are delivering a letter from Uncle Maury to Mrs. Patterson. They are not supposed to let anyone see it. Neither Caddy nor Benjy understands, but you realize that Uncle Maury is having an affair with Mrs. Patterson.

Page 14: "*Mr Patterson was . . .*" (later date)
It must be spring, because Mr. Patterson is hoeing his garden. Benjy has come alone to deliver another letter. Mr. Patterson is able to grab it out of Benjy's hands before he can give it to Mrs. Patterson. Eventually you will find out what happened as a result.

Page 14: " 'They ain't nothing . . .' " (1928)
Luster is hunting for a quarter so that he can go to the show. He takes Benjy down to the branch, or stream, where people are washing clothes. Luster enters into a conversation with them and boasts that he whips Benjy when he bellows. (In fact, he doesn't.)

NOTE: The show becomes important in the later sections of the novel. Mean-spirited Jason, who had two tickets, dropped them in the stove rather than give one of them to Luster the night before these events took place. And later that same evening Quentin (the girl) will run off with one of the performers.

At the end of this scene, Benjy begins to play in the branch.

Page 19: ". . . and Roskus came . . ." (1898)
Playing in the branch in 1928 evokes images for Benjy of playing there as a child with his brothers and sister. This scene is easy to date because the children talk about how old they are. Caddy gets her dress wet and takes it off so it will dry. Quentin slaps her and she falls in the water, getting her

drawers muddy. Versh says that he is going to tell, and Caddy threatens to run away. Benjy begins to cry, and Caddy comforts him. Benjy feels she smells like trees. Jason, meanwhile, is playing by himself.

The scenes at the branch reveal personality characteristics in the Compson children that foretell the kind of adults they will become. Caddy, in this scene, is bossy and adventurous. In taking off her dress in front of Quentin and Versh, she is doing something a girl isn't supposed to do. Quentin seems extremely upset that Caddy has taken off her dress. When he slaps her, she slips and gets her drawers dirty. This suggests both Quentin's incestuous feelings for Caddy and her later promiscuity. It also suggests that Quentin may be partly responsible for the latter—just as she gets her drawers muddy because Quentin has hit her. Benjy cries because Caddy is dirty, although he quickly reassures himself that she smells the way she always does—that is, that she hasn't changed. Jason is isolated from the others.

Page 21: "What is the . . ." (1928)

Benjy is once again moaning about Caddy's muddy drawers in 1898. Luster remarks that Benjy thinks he still owns the pasture. That tells you that the pasture used to belong to the Compsons but has been sold. Later you'll find out that Mr. Compson sold it to pay for Caddy's wedding and for Quentin's first year at Harvard.

Page 22: "Roskus came and . . ." (1898)

Benjy's thoughts are temporarily interrupted by Luster's question but quickly return to 1898. Here he repeats the words that first appeared on page 19. Roskus calls the children in to supper. They follow him, talking about the water fight in the branch.

NOTE: Once again, the adults' personalities are revealed in the actions of the children. In this scene from their childhood, Jason threatens to tell on Quentin and Caddy; Caddy pretends not to care; and Quentin tries to protect Caddy, attempting to convince Jason not to tell. As adults, Jason is sneaky and likes to punish other people; Caddy pretends not to care about other people's reactions when she does things that are wrong; and Quentin still tries, without much success, to protect Caddy from the consequences of her own actions.

Note that Benjy is called Maury here. His name has not yet been changed.

Page 23: *"See you all . . ."* (1928)
Luster's comments temporarily interrupt Benjy's thoughts.

Page 23: " 'If we go . . .' " (1898)
The children leave the branch and begin to return to the house. Jason walks with his hands in his pockets, symbolizing that, as a grownup, he will only care about making money. Meanwhile, Roskus is milking the cow.

Page 23: *"The cows came . . ."* (April 1910)
The image of Roskus milking the cow in 1898 makes Benjy think of another scene with cows. This scene contains many strange, disordered images—of the cow jumping out of the barn and of Benjy's recol-

lection that "the barn wasn't there and we had to wait until it came back." You can't figure them out until you realize that T.P. and Benjy are drunk on champagne (T.P. calls it "sassprilluh"). He mentions a wedding, and you realize that it is Caddy's. Later, in Quentin's section, you learn that it took place in April 1910.

NOTE: In this scene, Quentin beats up T.P. Why does he do that? Is he upset because T.P. has made Benjy drunk? Later, in Quentin's section, you'll find out why Quentin is so upset by Caddy's wedding. And when Quentin hits a fellow Harvard student, you'll remember this early example of his capacity for violence.

Page 25: *"At the top ..."* (1898)
After Benjy gets drunk at Caddy's wedding, Versh carries him up the hill. That image slides into another of a time when Versh carries him up the hill after he played with the other children in the branch. Dilsey then gives the children supper. You can see that she knows how to manage them very well. You can also see that the children's grandmother has died, and that Mrs. Compson is upset.

Page 32: *"There was a ..."* (1910 or 1912)
The thought of his grandmother's death reminds Benjy of other deaths he has experienced. In the next few scenes he thinks about several of them: his father's, Quentin's, and Roskus's. The first scene probably refers to Mr. Compson's death, because there would not have been a fire when Quentin died in June. And there would have been no need

to keep Benjy away from the big house. "Taint no luck on this place," Roskus says to T.P.

Page 33: *"Taint no luck . . ."* (1910)
Roskus's words in 1912 echoed what he had said at the time of Quentin's death two years before. This time you can be sure that it is Quentin's death that is referred to, because Roskus notes that Benjy is fifteen years old. Roskus refers to two "signs" that the Compson family is cursed, Benjy's birth and now Quentin's death. He wonders what the third sign will be.

Page 35: *"Take him and . . ."* (1912)
This scene occurs at the time of or shortly before Mr. Compson's death. Once again there is a fire. You can tell that it is later than in the previous scene because Luster has been born. So has little Quentin, who was brought to Mississippi in 1911, a year after her uncle's death. Roskus says that baby Quentin's illegitimate birth is the "third sign" he expected.

Page 37: *"You can't go . . ."* (1912)
Benjy sees Mr. Compson's funeral cortege. T.P. takes him to look at the carriage with the body.

Page 38: *"Come on, Luster . . ."* (1928)
Luster, in the present, interrupts Benjy again. He takes away the golf ball that Benjy wants to play with.

Page 38: "Frony and T.P. . . ." (1898)
The golf ball he's not allowed to play with in 1928 makes Benjy think of T.P.'s jar of fireflies thirty years earlier. Death is also still on his mind. Frony asks whether the funeral has begun, and Versh

tells her that she's not supposed to tell the Compson children about it. Frony mentions the custom among blacks of "moaning" for the dead. She is waiting to see whether the Compsons will moan too.

Page 38: *They moaned at . . ."* (19—)
Dilsey moans and the dog howls. It seems fairly clear that Dilsey's husband Roskus has died.

Page 39: *" 'Oh.' Caddy said . . ."* (1898)
Caddy doesn't understand that her grandmother is dead.

Page 39: *"Dilsey moaned, and . . ."* (19—)
You are taken back again to the time of Roskus's death. Nothing in this scene tells you exactly what year it is. But Frony is doing the cooking and Luster is old enough to take care of Benjy. That suggests it is at least several years after Mr. Compson's death.

Page 39: *" 'I like to . . .' "* (1898)
Frony tells Caddy that her grandmother is dead. But all Caddy knows of death is that Nancy (a farm animal) fell in the ditch and had to be shot by Roskus. Then the buzzards ate her flesh.

Page 39: *"The bones rounded . . ."* (1912)
Benjy saw Nancy's bones on the night his father died. You can tell this passage is about Mr. Compson's death because Benjy mentions "Father was sick" and T.P. talks about forgetting Benjy's coat. He wouldn't have needed a coat when Quentin died in June. Once again, Benjy is able to smell death.

Page 4 *"I had it . . ."* **(1928)**
Luster's comments about the quarter interrupt
Benjy's thoughts.

Page 42: "Do you think . . ." **(1898)**
The children talk about buzzards, funerals, and
the fireflies. They decide to get closer to the house
to find out whether a party (as Caddy maintains)
or a funeral is going on.

Page 43: *"When we looked . . ."* **(1910)**
Peering into the house makes Benjy think of the
way he and T.P. looked in the windows to see if
Caddy's wedding had started. T.P. brings them a
bottle of "sassprilluh."

Page 44: "A snake crawled . . ." **(1898)**
On these next few pages, there are several rapid
alterations between scenes at the time of Damuddy's death and Caddy's wedding.

Page 44: *"You ain't got . . ."* **(1910)**
T.P. and Benjy begin drinking.

Page 44: "We stopped under . . ." **(1898)**
The children look at the windows of the house;
the party or funeral hasn't started yet.

Page 45: *"They getting ready . . ."* **(1910)**
The wedding is almost ready to begin, and already
T.P. is tipsy. He asks Benjy to peer in the window
and see if the ceremony has started.

Page 45: " 'They haven't started . . .' " **(1898)**
This line should probably be in italics, since it represents a time change. Perhaps an error was made
in preparing the first edition of *The Sound and the
Fury.*

Now the children, rather than T.P. and Benjy, are looking in the window and waiting for something to begin. Caddy asks Versh for a boost into the tree so she can get a better look. The children see Caddy's muddy drawers. This is the image that Faulkner said inspired him to write the novel.

Page 46: "*I saw them.*" (1910)
The wedding has begun, and through the window Benjy sees Caddy with flowers in her hair and a long veil. By now he and T.P. have been drinking for some time. T.P. is laughing drunkenly, and Benjy begins to cry. Then Quentin kicks T.P. and Caddy comes in her wedding dress to comfort Benjy. Benjy feels she no longer smells like trees.

NOTE: Caddy smells like trees to Benjy when she is being the loving little mother of Benjy's childhood. In the scenes that follow, her withdrawal from Benjy as she becomes sexually mature is connected with his feeling that she no longer smells like trees.

Page 48: "*Benjy, Caddy said . . .*" (1905 or 1906)
Caddy is growing up. Jason teases her for wearing what he calls a prissy dress and mentions that she is fourteen. Benjy is upset by something about Caddy, and she can't figure out what it is. Finally she realizes that he doesn't like her to wear perfume. She washes it off and gives the bottle to Dilsey for a present. Then Benjy feels she smells like trees again.

Page 51: " 'Come on, now.' " (1908)
Benjy is now thirteen. Dilsey says that he is big
enough for his own bedroom. Uncle Maury's room
will be given to him.

Page 51: "Uncle Maury was . . ." (19—)
There is no indication in the text that the time has
changed, but in this scene you are back at the end-
ing of Uncle Maury's affair with Mrs. Patterson.
(See page 14 in the novel for Mr. Patterson's in-
terception of Uncle Maury's letter to his wife.) Mr.
Patterson has given Uncle Maury a black eye, and
Uncle Maury threatens to shoot him.

Page 53: " 'You a big . . .' " (1908)
Again there is no indication of a time change, but
here you are back in 1908 when Benjy is being put
to sleep in Uncle Maury's room. He is frantic because he is not allowed to sleep with Caddy any
longer. Caddy lies down with him so that he can
go to sleep. She still smells like trees to him.

Page 53: "We looked up . . ." (1898)
Caddy is in the tree, watching the funeral. Dilsey
discovers the children and brings them back into
the house.

Page 55: *"Where you want . . ."* (1928)
The scene shifts back to the present for a moment.

**Page 55: "The kitchen was . . ." (some time
between 1906 and 1909)**
On a moonlit night, Benjy slips away from T.P.
and goes outside.

Page 56: *"Luster came back."* (1928)
Luster tries to steer Benjy away from the swing
where Caddy's daughter Quentin is lounging with
a boy.

Page 56: "It was dark . . ." (19—)
Benjy looks out at the swing and begins to cry.

Page 56: "*Come away from . . .*" (1928)
Luster is still trying to get Benjy away from the swing. While heading toward it in 1928, Benjy thinks about an episode that occurred on the swing about twenty years earlier.

Page 56: "*It was two . . .*" (19—)
Benjy sees Caddy and her boyfriend Charlie on the swing. She gets off and comes to talk to him. Charlie is nasty to Benjy and asks Caddy to send Benjy away, but, instead, Caddy and Benjy run away from Charlie. Caddy washes her mouth out with soap. After she has done so, she smells like trees again to Benjy.

NOTE: Benjy is upset when Caddy spends time with boys. And apparently he has the power to make Caddy feel guilty about her sexuality. Thus she washes off the perfume and washes her mouth out with soap after she's kissed Charlie. Apparently she's able to purify herself to Benjy's satisfaction, because she smells again like trees to him. After she loses her virginity, she will never again smell like trees to Benjy.

Page 58: "*I kept a . . .*" (1928)
Benjy approaches Caddy's daughter Quentin and a man on the swing. This reminds you of the time he found Caddy and Charlie on the swing. But things have changed. While Charlie wanted Benjy to go away, Quentin's friend is really cruel to him.

And while Benjy was upset to find Caddy kissing Charlie, he doesn't care what Quentin does. At the same time, Quentin has no feeling for Benjy.

You won't understand the significance of this scene until Jason's section of the novel. But the man in the red tie belongs to the show that Luster wants to see. This is Saturday afternoon. Late that night, Quentin will run away with him. From Luster's conversation with the man in the red tie, you learn that Quentin frequently climbs down the tree next to her window to go out with various men. (You may wonder whether it is the same tree her mother, Caddy, climbed thirty years before.) Looking on the ground for his lost quarter, Luster finds a condom under a bush. He gives it to Benjy to play with. The man in the red tie is upset.

NOTE: Caddy and Quentin in the swing   This episode underlines the difference between Caddy and her daughter. Caddy felt guilty when Benjy found her and Charlie kissing in the swing, but Quentin doesn't care. All she wants to do is to tell her grandmother that Benjy has been "spying" on her. Caddy was just kissing a boy, but Quentin has apparently had sex with lots of men. The fact that they use prophylactics suggests that they are not boys who get carried away by passion. On the other hand, Quentin is unlikely to get pregnant the way her mother did.

Benjy walks to the fence, with Luster trailing him. They see some girls with schoolbags coming home from school.

Page 62: "*You cant do . . .*" (1910)
Benjy is again waiting at the gate for Caddy to
come home from school. But T.P. reminds him that
Caddy has married and left home. Remember that
on pages 5–6 Versh told Caddy (in about 1902) that
nobody could keep Benjy away from the gate when
she was due home.

Watching the schoolgirls walking by the gate,
Benjy wants to talk to them—possibly to tell them
how much he misses Caddy. "I tried to say," he
puts it, which suggests that he can only make
noises, not form words. The girls are frightened
and cross to the other side of the street.

Page 63: "*How did he . . .*" (1910)
Sometime (either the same day or several weeks
later), Benjy has gotten past the gate. In response
to his father's questions, Jason denies that he left
it open. Jason suggests that Mr. Compson send
Benjy to Jackson—which you will learn later is the
state mental asylum—but Mr. Compson won't listen. .

Page 63: "It was open . . ." (1910)
Someone left the gate open. It may very well have
been Jason, although he denies it. Jason may have
done it deliberately, to force Mr. Compson to send
Benjy away.

The girls walking by the Compson house see
Benjy. One of them explains that he isn't danger-
ous. Then Benjy opens the gate and catches one
of the girls. (The Compsons eventually have Benjy
castrated, apparently fearing that his actions
stemmed from sexual inclinations.)

Page 64: "*Here, loony, Luster . . .*" (1928)
The thought of Caddy, or of being castrated, makes
Benjy bellow. On the golf course, Luster tries to

sell the ball he found. The white golfer won't buy it but takes it away—just as Benjy's testicles were taken away from him. Luster tells Benjy that when his mother dies, Jason will put him in the asylum in Jackson.

NOTE: When Benjy was a child, he was generally treated kindly. Caddy and Dilsey were good to him, and so were Mr. Compson and Versh. Although T.P. got him drunk at Caddy's wedding, he was also a sympathetic caretaker.

As he has grown older, Benjy has lost everyone who treated him well except Dilsey. The contrast between Versh or T.P. and Luster echoes the contrast between Caddy and Quentin. Versh or T.P. or Caddy might sometimes be annoyed by the responsibility of caring for Benjy, but they saw him as a fellow human being who had feelings. Quentin and Luster did not. There may be some suggestion that the younger generation, either black or white, is shallow and lacking in humanity.

Dilsey calls Luster and Benjy to the house. Knowing that the sight of fire calms Benjy down, she opens the firedoor in the stove.

Page 67: "*What you want . . .*" (1900)
The fire in the stove in 1928 evokes an image in Benjy's mind of a fire in his mother's room in 1900. She was telling him that he had a new name.

Page 68: " 'Aint you shamed . . .' " (1928)
Dilsey scolds Luster for teasing Benjy, and Luster talks back to her. He has no respect for his grand-

mother. His only concern now is obtaining a quarter so he can attend the show. Dilsey serves a birthday cake to Benjy and Luster. Benjy cries when Luster blows out the candles.

Page 69: "*I could hear . . .*" (probably 1900)
This scene is not dated. It is probably 1900, because it contains rain and a fire, like the other scenes from 1900.

Page 69: "I ate some . . ." (1928)
Benjy eats a piece of cake while Luster has two. Luster closes the door on the stove, making the fire disappear, and Benjy cries. Dilsey tells him to leave Benjy alone.

Page 70: "*That's right, Dilsey . . .*" (1900)
Dilsey asks Caddy why Maury's name has been changed to Benjamin. As far as she can see, changing a name doesn't accomplish anything. Dilsey's simple, dignified faith—she knows her name, who she is, and that she'll be called on judgment day—contrasts with that of the Compsons.

Page 71: "The long wire . . ." (1928)
Contrary to Dilsey's orders, Luster closes the firedoor again. Reaching out for the vanished fire, Benjy burns his hand. His bellowing rouses Mrs. Compson, who complains that Dilsey has let Benjy make noise in order to disturb her. Luster takes Benjy into the library and builds him a fire. But Benjy focuses instead on a dark place on the wall, and he tightly clutches a slipper. We'll soon learn that a mirror used to hang on that wall and that the slipper belonged to Caddy.

Page 74: "*Your name is . . .*" (1900)
Caddy informs Maury that his name has been
changed to Benjy. She tries to carry him.

Page 74: "Caddy said. 'Let . . .' " (1898)
The image of Caddy's carrying him makes Benjy
think of another time she tried to do so, at the time
of their grandmother's death.

Page 75: "*Versh set me . . .*" (1900)
The children are in their mother's room. Benjy can
see both the fire in the fireplace and its reflection
in the mirror. He imagines his mother's sickness
sitting on the cloth on her forehead.

Page 76: "*Mother's sick, Father . . .*" (1898)
The image of Mrs. Compson's being sick links
Benjy's thoughts of his grandmother's death in 1898
with his name change in 1900. Mrs. Compson's
response to any stress is to be "sick." In this scene,
Jason appears with his hands in his pockets once
again.

Page 76: "*We could hear . . .*" (1900)
Mrs. Compson yells at Caddy for carrying Benjy,
and accuses her and Mr. Compson of spoiling him.
She calls Caddy "Candace" and Benjy "Benjamin," insisting that nicknames are only for common people. Mrs. Compson insists that Caddy take
away the cushion Benjy is playing with happily.
Later, Mr. Compson comes in, and Benjy feels he
smells like rain. Caddy and Jason are fighting because Jason has cut up all the dolls Caddy made
for Benjy. Jason, even as a little boy, is bent on
destroying everyone else's happiness. But Caddy
promises to make more dolls.

Page 79: "*Jason came in.*" (1928)
Jason comes home in a bad mood. He tells Luster
to keep Benjy quiet. He has a nasty word for his
mother too.

Page 80: "*You can look . . .*" (1900)
Caddy had given Benjy everything that makes him
happy: a fire, a mirror, and a cushion. Jason can
be heard crying far away.

Page 80: "Dilsey said, 'You . . .' " (1928)
Dilsey calls Jason and his niece Quentin to supper.

Page 80: "*We could hear . . .*" (1900)
Quentin is complaining about the rain, as Caddy
did earlier. He has been fighting.

Page 81: "Quentin said, 'Didn't . . .' " (1928)
Luster asks Jason for a quarter. Later, when you
read Jason's section, you'll find out that Jason
burned two tickets to the show rather than give
one of them to Luster. So it's pathetic that Luster
asks Jason for money now. Caddy's daughter
Quentin comes down to supper heavily made up.
Jason warns her to stay away from the show people, but you know she's preparing to run off with
one of them.

Page 82: "*I could hear . . .*" (1900)
Mr. Compson asks Quentin about the fight. It turns
out that he hit another boy who had threatened to
put a frog in a girl's desk. (Even as a little boy,
Quentin is protecting girls from boys, as he will
later attempt to do for Caddy.) As Mr. Compson
points out, though, it's a little silly. Where would
the other boy find a frog in November?

Page 83: "*Dilsey said, All . . .*" (1928)
Dilsey calls everyone to supper.

Page 83: "*Versh smelled like . . .*" (1900)
Versh enters, wet from and smelling like the rain.

Page 83: "We could hear . . ." (about 1909)
Caddy comes in, probably from a date. She avoids
her parents and Benjy. Benjy, crying, tries to grab
her. She cries too. (Quentin also recalls this scene,
but in greater detail; page 185).

Page 84: "*Versh said, Your . . .*" (1900)
Versh tells Benjy a folk tale that proves that changing people's names is bad luck. Like Dilsey, he
doesn't think it's a good idea.

Page 84: "We were in . . ." (about 1909)
Benjy pushes Caddy into the bathroom. He is trying
to get her to wash herself clean, as she did after
she kissed Charlie in the swing. You can guess that
Caddy has lost her virginity. This is clearer in
Quentin's recollections.

Page 85: "*What are you . . .*" (1928)
Caddy's daughter, Quentin, complaining about
Benjy, says that he ought to be sent to Jackson. If
you don't like it here, you can get out, Jason tells
her. Don't worry, I will, she replies.

NOTE: When you read Jason's section, remember this scene. Quentin is telling the truth. She
plans to leave home that night. Although Benjy
doesn't understand what is going on, you can see
that he observes many interactions that turn out
to be important.

Page 85: "Versh said, 'You . . .' " (1900)
Caddy offers to feed Benjy supper.

Page 86: *"Has he got . . ."* (1928)

Page 86: *"Steam came off . . ."* (1900)

Page 86: *"Now, now, Dilsey . . ."* (1928)

Page 86: *"It got down . . ."* (1900)

Page 86: *"Yes he will . . ."* (1928)

Page 86: *"Roskus said, 'It . . .' "* (1900)

Page 86: *"You've been running . . ."* (1928)

Page 86: " 'Then I don't . . .' " (1900)
The quickly alternating scenes on Page 86 contrast
the warm world of 1900 with the brutal present.
In 1900, Caddy fed Benjy while rain pounded on
the roof. In the present, her daughter Quentin criticizes his eating habits. She accuses him again of
spying on her.

Page 87: *"Oh, I wouldn't . . ."* (1928)
Dilsey comforts Quentin and says it's not fair of
Jason to blame her for her illegitimate birth.

Page 87: " 'She sulling again . . .' " (1900)
Roskus remarks that Mrs. Compson is sulking in
her room. Dilsey shushes him.

Page 87: *"Quentin pushed Dilsey . . ."* (1928)
But Quentin is unable to accept Dilsey's love. You'll
see her act this way again in Jason's section. Dilsey
tries unsuccessfully to arbitrate between Quentin
and Jason.

Page 87: " 'Mother's sick again . . .' " (1900)

Page 87: "*Goddamn you, Quentin . . .*" (1928)
In these two scenes, Caddy's solicitousness for others is contrasted with her daughter Quentin's meanness.

Page 87: "Caddy gave me . . ." (1900)
Mr. Compson and the children are together. There's a fire in the fireplace. Caddy gives Benjy a cushion to hold. She smells like trees to him.

Page 88: "*She smelled like . . .*" (1928)
Benjy clutches the slipper that is all he has left of Caddy. Caddy's daughter gives Luster a quarter so that he can go to the show.

Page 89: "We didn't go . . ." (1898)
The children are put to bed in a different room because of their grandmother's death.

Page 89: "*Quentin, Mother said . . .*" (1928)
Mrs. Compson complains because Dilsey doesn't bring her hot water bottle quickly enough.

Page 90: "Quentin and Versh . . ." (1900)
Quentin comes in, crying.

Page 90: "*I got undressed . . .*" (1928)
Looking at himself as he undresses, Benjy cries as he thinks about his castration. He and Luster see Caddy's daughter climbing down the tree. Its shaking recalls the way the tree shook when Caddy climbed it in 1898 to watch Damuddy's funeral. This is the last anyone in the novel will see of Quentin.

Page 90: "There were two . . ." (1900)
The last scene in this section returns to Benjy's earliest memory, Damuddy's death. The children

are put to bed, and Benjy falls asleep, secure in the love and order around him. This image contrasts violently with our last sight of Benjy at the novel's end.

JUNE SECOND 1910 (QUENTIN'S SECTION)

Having made it through Benjy's section, you'll find Quentin's both easier and more difficult. It's easier because the memories of Quentin—who may act foolishly but is very intelligent—are more coherent than Benjy's. In addition, Quentin remembers some of the same things Benjy does. You'll recognize the episode with T.P. and the "sassprilluh" at Caddy's wedding, or the scene when Benjy drags Caddy into the bathroom. Quentin also remembers Caddy's muddy drawers and seeing Nancy's bones in the ditch.

On the other hand, Quentin's section is longer, more obscure, and more packed with images and fragmented ideas than Benjy's. Quentin's mind, like his brother's, is largely in the past as he makes his daily rounds in the present. But whereas places and sensations in the present—the fence, the fire—propelled Benjy back into the past, Quentin's memories need no prompting. Occasionally something in the present will remind him of the past. For example, he hits Gerald Bland, a Harvard student, because Gerald says something that reminds him of Caddy's seducer, Dalton Ames. But basically Quentin is thinking about one thing—Caddy's sexuality. Sometimes he remembers the first time she kissed a boy. Other times he thinks about her loss of virginity. He also remembers the night before her wedding and the wedding itself.

Quentin's mind works more quickly than Benjy's, so the shifts in time in his section are much more frequent. Quentin often thinks in fragments of sentences. Sometimes his mind jumps back and forth between the present and the past. Other times it moves among several different memories. Quentin frequently repeats words ("Dalton Ames") or phrases ("the voice that breathed"). Sometimes he remembers only part of a memory that is not fully explained until later in the section. For example, the line "one moment she was standing" appears several times before the memory is fully developed toward the end of the section. In some passages, a half dozen memories are strung together. But beware: Not all time shifts are signaled by changes in typeface.

As you read Quentin's section, watch for scenes that you remember from Benjy's section. Often Quentin presents the same events in ways that make a lot more sense. Reading Quentin's memories, you'll be able to go back and understand what Benjy was talking about. Other times, Quentin also knows more than Benjy. Benjy, to take one example, remembers the night that Caddy came home after having had sex with Dalton Ames. But after Benjy has been put to bed, Quentin has a conversation with her. Benjy only knew that something was very wrong. Quentin feels the same way, but he lets you know what happened and how Caddy felt about it.

Be alert, too, to the words Quentin uses most often. His section is filled with references to time (watches, clocks, chimes), shadows, water, sisters, and honeysuckle. These recurring images are keys to Quentin's thoughts. When Benjy saw water, it was usually just water. Things had associations for him (fire was associated with a sense of security), but he was not capable of thinking that something was like something else. For Quentin, however, water is never simply water, but has symbolic importance.

NOTE: Events in Quentin's section   Quentin has a number of relatively unimportant memories (of breaking his leg, of reading a picture book, of Jason and the Patterson boy going into a kite-making "business") that cannot be dated. The following memories, listed in chronological order, are the most significant.

- Damuddy's death (1898)
- Benjy's name change (1900)
- Kissing Natalie (undated)
- Caddy kissing a boy (1906–1907)
- Caddy having sex with Dalton Ames (late summer 1909)
- Wedding announcement (1910)
- Meeting Herbert (April 22, 1910)
- Wedding eve (April 23, 1910)
- Wedding (April 24, 1910)

Pages 93–98
Quentin awakens in his Harvard dorm on the morning of June 2, 1910. He can tell time by the shadows on his curtains and does not need to look at his watch, which was once his grandfather's.

His roommate, Shreve, warns him he'll be late for chapel.

As he wakes up, Quentin thinks about (1) the passage of time and his father's ideas on the subject; (2) Christ and St. Francis; (3) sisters; (4) Caddy's wedding; (5) Caddy's wedding announcement; (6) a conversation he had with his father on the night she lost her virginity; (7) Mr. Compson's comments on virginity; (8) a quarrel he had with Spoade, a Harvard acquaintance, about women; and (9) committing suicide.

Let's look closely at one paragraph—the first one on page 95—to see how this works. Quentin is thinking about what a nice day it is and how good the weather is for the Harvard crew's boat race later that day. It is June, the month of marriages. The lines *"She ran right out of the mirror . . ."* are a memory of Caddy's wedding. Next he thinks of Caddy's wedding announcement: *"Mr and Mrs Jason Richmond Compson announce . . ."* He then thinks of the roses at her wedding—they are red, not virginal white like dogwood blossoms. "I said I have committed incest, Father I said" is a memory of a conversation Quentin had with his father on the night that Caddy lost her virginity (see pages 219–22 in the novel for a fuller account of this conversation). Then his mind returns to the boat race. Unlike Benjy, whose mind calls up one scene at a time, Quentin has run several memories together in the course of a minute.

The conversation with his father about Caddy (he claims that Caddy had slept with him, not Dalton Ames) is described at slightly greater length on pages 97–98. This memory is interrupted by a startling image: "And I will look down and see my

murmuring bones and the deep water like wind
. . ." Quentin is picturing his death by drowning.

Pages 98–105
Quentin smashes the face of his watch, cutting his
thumb, and then pulls off the hands of the watch.
He paints the cut with iodine. Then he packs his
trunk, keeping out two changes of clothing, locks
it, and addresses it. He writes and seals two notes.
Quentin then goes looking for Deacon, a black man
he wants to run an errand for him, but can't find
him. He has breakfast and visits a jeweler's shop,
where he talks about watches. Then he goes to a
hardware store to buy flat-irons. Because he has
earlier imagined his bones in deep water and
thought "on the Day when He says Rise only the
flat-iron would come floating up" (p. 98), we realize that Quentin will use the flat-irons in his suicide.

NOTE: Time   Quentin's section has many references to time. In these first ten pages, Quentin
tells time by the shadow, listens to the ticking of
his watch, smashes the face of the watch, listens
to the college chimes, and brings the watch to a
jewelry store whose window is filled with watches.
Between memories of Caddy's wedding, Quentin
is thinking about his father's pronouncements on
the subject of time. On giving him the watch, Mr.
Compson called it "the mausoleum of all hope and
desire." He said, "I give it to you not that you may
remember time, but that you might forget it now
and then for a moment and not spend all your
breath trying to conquer it." Mr. Compson says
that no one ever accomplishes anything. Later,

Quentin recalls Mr. Compson's comment that Christ
"was worn away by a minute clicking of little
wheels." That is, the demands of daily life are killing. Quentin wants to know whether any of the
watches in the jeweler's window show the right
time, but he doesn't want to know what it is.
Quentin wants to live in a world without time.

Throughout this section, Quentin will ask people where there's a clock (the boys fishing in the
river, for example) and will listen for the chimes.
Being time-bound is the human tragedy, Mr.
Compson suggests ("only when the clock stops
does time come to life"; page 105). But Quentin
wants to stop the clock, not to bring time to life,
but to die.

Pages 105–19
On a streetcar to the river, Quentin sits next to a
black man and thinks about his feelings toward
blacks. When he sees his shadow in the water, he
imagines it drowned. The Harvard crew comes out
of the boathouse. One of its members is Gerald
Bland, a man he knows. Gerald's mother drives
by to pick him up. Mrs. Bland, who has taken an
apartment in Cambridge to be close to her son,
likes to boast about his conquests of women.

While these events are occurring in the present,
Quentin has other thoughts. He remembers kissing a girl ("*Moving sitting still*"), a memory that will
be explored at greater length on pages 167–72. He
remembers Caddy standing in the door on the night
she lost her virginity. He also remembers the children playing in the branch the night of Damuddy's
death. Compare this recollection ("*I'm going to run*

away"; page 109) with Benjy's account of the same incident (page 21). He remembers the changing of Benjy's name and the comment that changing his name won't change his luck (see Benjy's recollection of the same comment; page 71). While he is thinking about his own death, Quentin remembers that Benjy smelled Damuddy's death. His recollection of a conversation with Dalton Ames on page 113 (*"Did you ever have a sister?"*) will be reproduced at length on pages 185 and 197. Quentin also remembers his mother's wishes for him to go to Harvard and the first time Caddy kisses a boy. You recognize his recollection of Benjy's behavior at Caddy's wedding (*"He was lying beside the box under the window"*; page 114) from Benjy's account on page 47.

In a long section (pages 114–16), Quentin remembers meeting Herbert, the man Caddy marries. Here you learn for the first time that Herbert has promised Jason a job in his bank. Herbert has given Caddy a car for a present. Mrs. Compson is thrilled with the car and with Herbert, and she goes on about it (pages 115–16) in the pretentious manner you can identify as unmistakably hers.

Other memories on these pages include one of Jason and the Patterson boy (the son of the woman Uncle Maury had the affair with, in Benjy's section) making kites together. (This foretells Jason's future in business.) Quentin also remembers his father's selling the pasture so he can go to Harvard. And he thinks back yet another time to the discussion about incest. He replays a conversation in which his mother accuses him of spying on Caddy. Finally, he recalls a conversation about women with his father (women have *"an affinity for evil,''* his father says). Quentin thinks to himself that "Father and I protect women."

Pages 119–39
In these pages, Quentin finds Deacon and hands him the letter to give to Shreve. By now we realize that the letters he wrote are suicide notes. Back in his room, he and Shreve discuss Gerald Bland and his mother.

His thoughts, however, are elsewhere. Quentin remembers a number of scenes you recall from Benjy's section: Benjy drunk at Caddy's wedding, Uncle Maury drinking at Christmastime (the Patterson episode), and Jason keeping his hands in his pockets and falling down. These pages also contain a recollection of a long monologue by Mrs. Compson when Caddy loses her virginity.

Quentin also remembers the night before Caddy's wedding: his fantasy that he shot Herbert (page 130), Caddy's request that he look after Benjy and Father (page 131), and Caddy's telling him that she is sick (page 131). You'll soon understand why. On pages 133–38, there is a lengthy recollection of his meeting with Herbert. Herbert tried to treat him like a regular guy, making crude jokes about women, much to Quentin's horror.

Pages 139–55
Quentin walks along the river, still watching his shadow in the water. He meets some boys who are trying to catch a famous fish so large that there is a prize for catching it. They discuss what they'll do with the prize money, but it's clear they don't really want to catch it. Some readers believe this is a comment on Quentin's relationship with Caddy.

Caddy is still the focus of Quentin's thoughts as

he walks along. He recalls at length the scene in which Caddy stands at the door, with Benjy pulling at her dress (for Benjy's memory, see page 82), on the night she lost her virginity. Several notable memories occur in these pages. In answer to Quentin's repeated question about how many boys she's slept with, Caddy responds, *"There was something terrible in me."* The night before her wedding, she makes Quentin promise not to let the family send Benjy to Jackson. Quentin asks her why she's marrying a "blackguard" like Herbert and tells Caddy that Herbert had been expelled from prep school. Caddy explains she had to marry someone because she's pregnant. Quentin offers to run away with her and Benjy, but Caddy asks what they'll do for money.

There are two other important memories in these pages. One is Quentin's recollection of a story Versh told him about a man mutilating himself. This may be a memory of Benjy's castration. But Quentin thinks, "But that's not it. It's not not having them," and then recalls a conversation with his father about his own virginity. The castrated man Quentin is thinking about is probably himself. The other important image is Quentin's fantasy of incest with Caddy. The two of them are beyond hell together, protected by a *"clean flame"* (pages 144–45).

NOTE: Quentin and shadows Quentin constantly sees shadows. He notices the shadows of all the objects around him. He is also aware of his own shadow—he steps on it, tries to trick it, imagines it drowned. Quentin's obsession with shadows points to one of the themes Faulkner exam-

ines in *The Sound and the Fury*: what is real and
what is only a shadow? One way of approaching
the theme is to say Quentin lives in the shadow of
the past. Certainly his memories of Caddy are much
more real to him than his preparations for suicide.
As you may have noticed in this discussion, Quentin's actions in the present can usually be sum-
marized in a line or two; his memories are much
fuller and richer. It could also be said that Quentin
is a pale copy of a normal man, like a shadow. He
is still a virgin and doesn't seem to like sex very
much. In addition to being asexual, he never seems
actually to carry out any of his fantasies. As you'll
see later, he doesn't shoot Dalton Ames when he
has the chance. He doesn't make love to Caddy.
When he fights with Gerald Bland—mistaking him
for Ames—he lets Bland beat him up. Quentin is
not capable of acting very effectively in the world.

The frequent mention of shadows recalls Macbeth's statement that "Life's but a walking shadow."
Quentin's life certainly is.

Pages 155–86
A ragged little Italian girl follows Quentin into a
bakery. He calls her "sister" and buys her something to eat. Then, for hours, while she follows
him around, he tries to figure out where she lives.

Being with the girl evokes memories in Quentin.
He remembers once again his father's remarks about
women. He also remembers how he slapped Caddy
the first time she kissed a boy. That, in turn, brings
to mind the first time he kissed a girl, whose name
was Natalie. He thought of her as dirty.

Eventually, the Italian girl's brother, Julio, ap-

pears with a local constable and accuses Quentin
of kidnapping his sister. At that moment, Gerald
Bland, his mother, Shreve, and some friends drive
up. They testify to Quentin's character, and Quentin is fined six dollars and let off.

The episode strikes Quentin as dreadfully funny.
Julio's threats to kill Quentin are a parody of
Quentin's threats against Dalton Ames. More significantly, Julio is a man who has strong feelings
about his sister. Instead of recognizing Quentin as
a kindred spirit, Julio attacks him.

In the car with his friends, Quentin remembers
again Caddy's explanation that her promiscuity was
caused by *"something terrible in me."* When he asked
her if she loved the men she slept with, Caddy
replied, *"When they touched me I died."* Quentin tells
Caddy he'll convince their father that it was he,
not Dalton Ames, who had slept with her. In these
pages, descriptions of sexual activity are always
accompanied by the smell of honeysuckle.

Pages 186–203
Quentin recalls at some length the events surrounding Caddy's loss of her virginity. The smell
of honeysuckle is so overpowering that Quentin
can barely breathe. Sitting by the branch, Caddy
and Quentin talk. Quentin reminds her of the time
she got her drawers muddy (for Benjy's account,
see page 21) and wonders if they can still see Nancy's bones (which Benjy sees on pages 40–41). He
suggests that he cut both their throats, and Caddy
agrees, but he is unable to do it. Later, she agrees
to sleep with him, and he backs away. He tells her
that *"theres a curse on us its not our fault."*

Several days later, Quentin confronts Dalton

Ames, the man Caddy had sex with. He refuses
to leave town, as Quentin requests. Quentin asks
him if he ever had a sister, and when Dalton replies, "no but theyre all bitches," Quentin hits him.
Dalton demonstrates his skill with a pistol and then
puts it in Quentin's hand. But Quentin cannot pull
the trigger. Instead he faints—"like a girl," he realizes later.

Pages 203–14
Back in the country scene again, Shreve tells
Quentin, who doesn't quite remember what happened, that when Gerald was boasting about his
women, Quentin jumped up and said, "Did you
ever have a sister?" and hit him. Quentin clearly
confused Gerald with Dalton Ames. And just as
Dalton Ames was a better shot than Quentin, Gerald is a better boxer. In the twilight Quentin takes
a trolley back to school.

NOTE: Incest It may be hard to identify with
Quentin's obsession with Caddy's virginity. Would
most brothers today be so upset if their sisters, by
their own choice, slept with a boyfriend? (And
would most mothers dress in black the day after
their daughter first kissed a boy, as Mrs. Compson
did?) Even Benjy gets into the act, crying and drag-
ging Caddy into the bathroom so she can wash
herself.

But Quentin's strong feelings about his sister—
and hers about him—seem less unusual. Perhaps,
like Quentin, you too have an especially warm or
close tie with a brother or sister. And you may
recognize and sympathize with Quentin's anger at
the men who seem to him to be taking Caddy away.

Quentin remembers Benjy sitting in front of a
mirror, and Dilsey saying that Mrs. Compson was
too proud for him (a comment Versh makes in
Benjy's section). He also remembers falling asleep
as a child.

Back in his room, as he cleans the blood off his
tie with gasoline (pages 213–14), Quentin's thoughts
rush by. He thinks of Caddy with the first car in
town, and of Benjy, then thinks again, "*if I'd just
had a mother.*"

Pages 214–22
Quentin is making the final preparations for his
suicide. "A quarter hour yet. And then I'll not be.
The peacefullest words." Washing his face and
brushing his teeth, he dresses neatly.

His thoughts are flying thick and fast. He remembers Caddy's wedding, the wedding announcement, the sale of the pasture, Caddy standing in the door and Benjy crying (at the loss of her
virginity), and Caddy's accusation that he was
spying on her. Again he recalls his father's dis-
missive comments about women. He remembers
his father's nasty comments about Uncle Maury
and his mother's defense of him. He also recalls
his grandfather: "Grandfather wore his uniform
and we could hear the murmur of their voices . . .
Grandfather was always right." This ancestral cer-
tainty is gone for good.

Finally, Quentin remembers his final conversation with his father about incest. Mr. Compson
understands why Quentin wanted to believe he'd
committed incest with Caddy. But to Mr. Compson, Caddy's loss of virginity is no tragedy. He
tells Quentin that "you cannot bear to think that
someday it will no longer hurt you like this," and

suggests that Quentin leave for Harvard a little early.

Making sure that everything is in perfect order, Quentin leaves the room and heads for the river.

NOTE: The last remembered conversation with Mr. Compson explains one of the motivations for Quentin's suicide. Quentin had tried to inflate Caddy's virginity into something crucial. Imagining that he had taken it—that the two of them had committed incest—was a way of making it important. The two of them would be damned, in a special part of hell. But Mr. Compson says, in effect, you'll get over it. Quentin doesn't want to get over it. As his father's final comment suggests, for Quentin "was" is the saddest word. Only the past is lovable, beautiful, or real. The only way to give life meaning is to end it.

Given all the facts you now have about Quentin, was the river the only option for him? Why can't Quentin see any other possibilities? Can you imagine Quentin, having decided against suicide, as an older man? What would his role in the family have been if he had lived?

APRIL SIXTH 1928
(JASON'S SECTION)

Jason's section of *The Sound and the Fury* is entirely different from Benjy's and Quentin's. Jason's memories of the past are not as vivid as they are for his two brothers. Jason's voice is very different too. While Benjy's voice is calm and gentle, and

Quentin's impassioned and convoluted, Jason's voice is hurried, nasty, and vulgar. In the section Jason narrates, we see that Mrs. Compson is right: he is not like anyone else in the family.

Jason's main interests are in the present. He is most concerned with his continuing battles with his niece, Quentin, and his cotton brokers in New York. In the course of his narration, you'll hear and see a lot about the kind of person Jason is. But you'll also find out what happened after Quentin died and Herbert Head kicked Caddy out. And you'll learn about some complicated financial double-dealing.

Jason's day—April 6, 1928, Good Friday—begins with a fight about Quentin. Mrs. Compson is concerned because the girl's been cutting school. Typically, her real worry is not about her granddaughter, but what the school authorities will think. Jason goes to the kitchen and grabs the girl by the arm. Dilsey tries to prevent Jason from beating her, but Quentin doesn't appreciate her protection, calling Dilsey a nigger and telling her to get away. Quentin and Jason fight about money. Jason claims he is supporting her, while Quentin says the money she lives on comes from her mother. Jason implies Mrs. Compson burns all Caddy's checks. Quentin is not ashamed of her behavior: "I'm bad and I'm going to hell, and I don't care," she says.

NOTE: In Jason's constant attention to the way Quentin looks—her lipstick, her makeup, her dresses, the way she does her hair—and in the scene where her kimono falls open, revealing her breasts, there is some suggestion of sexual attrac-

tion between uncle and niece. If so, this would be
an ironic echo of the attraction between Caddy and
her brother Quentin. It is interesting that Jason is
so hard on his niece Quentin in light of the fact
(which will emerge later in the section) that he is
keeping a mistress in Memphis. "I've got every
respect for a good honest whore," he explains (page
291). But when he calls Quentin a "little whore"
(page 269), the respect apparently does not extend
to her. He is also unforgiving of Caddy. He seems
to have special anger at the women in his family.

Jason's meanness is not limited to the members
of his immediate family. When he gets to work,
he is nasty to Uncle Job, an old man who works
for his boss, Earl. And, talking to a traveling salesman, he makes cracks about the Jews. Jason plays
the cotton market, and worries that other people
have inside information. His view of the business
world is identical to his view of his family: everyone else gets all the good stuff. Jason's frenzied
efforts to keep up with the cotton market—his feeling that he's being played for a sucker by brokers
in New York and that the clerks at the local West-
ern Union office are withholding information from
him—are a major focus of this section.

At the store, Jason receives a letter from Caddy,
who asks tenderly about Quentin. It is clear from
the letter that she cares about her daughter. It is
also clear that she has been giving Jason a fair
amount of money to pay for Quentin's keep.

Although Jason is always complaining about how
much he works (and about how his brother Quentin was sent to Harvard while he didn't receive a

college education), it doesn't seem that he works very much. Later you'll see Jason go home for a midday dinner in defiance of his boss. And he takes time off in the middle of the afternoon to go chasing after his niece Quentin and her boyfriend. His boss, Earl, a good-hearted man, keeps him on largely out of pity for Mrs. Compson. Jason, realizing this, keeps provoking Earl to fire him.

Jason's memories lack the vividness of Benjy's or Quentin's. Shortly after his son Quentin's funeral, Mr. Compson went north to pick up baby Quentin. Mr. Compson and Dilsey welcome the baby, but Mrs. Compson plans to raise her without ever speaking Caddy's name. (In Benjy's section, Roskus, Dilsey, and Frony talk about how awful this is; see page 37.) It turns out (page 274) Mr. Compson wanted to let Caddy come home when Herbert threw her out, but Mrs. Compson forbade it. Mrs. Compson has always been at war with Caddy's sexuality. Once when she caught Caddy kissing a boy, Mrs. Compson wore a black dress and veil the next day (page 286).

Jason remembers his father's funeral too. Once again, Uncle Maury was there, with his fawning manner and his outstretched hand. Walking away from the grave, Jason encountered a woman in a veil who turned out to be Caddy. Talking to Caddy at the funeral, Jason "got to thinking about when we were little and one thing and another and I got to feeling funny again, kind of mad or something." When she offers Jason fifty dollars to let her see baby Quentin, Jason agrees, and drives by her in a hired car, holding the baby up to the window for a moment. When Caddy complains, Jason threatens to tell their mother that she's been in town. Caddy reliably sends checks and clearly wants Quentin to be taken care of, but Jason won't let her see bank statements and prevents her from approaching Dilsey.

NOTE: Although Jason thinks that he can shuck off the past, he, too, is in its grip. He knows the difference between past and present in a way his brothers don't. But the past still colors Jason's priorities and views of the present. He is punitive toward his niece Quentin, nasty to the world, and paranoid about business, because of his feelings about his siblings. The memories may not dance before his eyes, but old feelings are still calling Jason's tune.

Caddy has sent Quentin a money order for fifty dollars over and above her support check in a letter that Jason opens. When the girl comes to the store to ask for the money, Jason tells her that Caddy has sent only ten dollars. Jason then leaves the store, although his boss has asked him to stay because it's a busy day. He stops by the telegraph office for news of the market, then hurries home.

For years, Jason has been pulling an elaborate financial scam on his mother. Mrs. Compson has been burning what she thinks are Caddy's support checks for Quentin. In reality, the checks she burns have been forged by Jason, and he has deposited the real checks in Mrs. Compson's bank account, pretending that they are his salary. He has used his own salary from the store for playing the market and for his Memphis women.

As he gives his mother the latest phony check, which replaces the money order from Caddy, Jason pretends to argue with her about the wisdom of destroying these checks. It turns out later that Jason has managed another deal as well. With the little money she inherited from her husband, Mrs. Compson bought Jason a share in the hardware store where he worked. Without telling her, Jason withdrew the money from the business to buy a car.

Returning to the store after lunch, Jason sees Quentin drive off with a man in a red tie. He follows them. When he leaves his car in a field to chase after them on foot, they let the air out of his tires. Jason returns to town in a fury and with a terrible headache, resentful both of Quentin and of "these damn little slick haired squirts."

NOTE: Because you have read the previous two sections, you know more than Jason does about some things. Having watched the way the man with the red tie treated Benjy (pages 59–60), you know that he really is rotten. And you also know that Jason's chase is in vain—Quentin will run off with him the following night.

Jason returns to the store for a few minutes, then stops at the telegraph office for one more nasty exchange with the clerks. Coming home, he finds Benjy at the gate. Jason sees Benjy as a butt for his jokes. He doesn't realize Benjy has feelings.

In the kitchen, waiting for dinner, Jason indulges in another mean act. Earl, his boss, has given him two free tickets to the show. Although Luster desperately wants to go, Jason will not give him a ticket. He offers to sell him one for money Luster doesn't have. Rather than give it to him, he burns it before Luster's eyes.

NOTE: Dilsey then gets Luster a quarter from Frony. Luster drops it on the golf course on Saturday morning. This is the background of Luster's frantic hunt for a quarter during Benjy's section. Saturday night is the last night of the show. In Jason's section, you see Jefferson is full of people waiting for the show. We understand Luster's sense of urgency.

After insisting that Quentin and his mother come down to dinner so that he can pick another fight, Jason goes off to his room to count his money before going to bed.

NOTE: A number of Jason's passing comments fill in gaps in what you learned in the previous two sections of *The Sound and the Fury*. For example, Jason notices Benjy going to a dark place on the wall where the mirror used to hang. That explains an action in Benjy's section on page 74. Jason also remembers that Mr. Burgess, the father of the little girl Benjy chased, hit him with a fence plank. Mrs. Compson's mention of Jason's allergy to gasoline on page 296 recalls Quentin's reference to it on page 213. Jason's section contains many such tidbits that increase the sense you probably have by now of really knowing the Compson family.

APRIL EIGHTH 1928

The last section of *The Sound and the Fury* is written by an omniscient author; that is, the person who is writing sees clearly, and more or less objectively, what is going on. However, the point of view stays close to that of Dilsey. In this section she emerges most clearly as the person who holds the family together (her goodness and strength were apparent earlier). For that reason, the section is often called Dilsey's section, even though it is not told in her voice.

Easter morning at the Compsons' begins with familiar scenes. Mrs. Compson, complaining that Dilsey isn't doing enough, gives her a half dozen contradictory orders. ("You're not the one who has to bear it," Mrs. Compson says to the woman who does.) Jason claims that the window in his bedroom is broken and blames it on Luster. Benjy sits at the table and moans. Dilsey moves about the kitchen, singing and preparing breakfast. When the clock strikes five, Dilsey says, "Eight o'clock," knowing that the clock is wrong.

NOTE: Dilsey's remark must be considered in the light of the other time imagery in *The Sound and the Fury*. Quentin, you remember, tore the hands off his watch and didn't want to know the time. In contrast, Dilsey knows what time it is even if the clock is wrong. Her comment shows Dilsey's ability to distinguish between the present and the past. Later the ticking of the clock is likened to "the dry pulse of the decaying house itself." Here, the passage of time is connected to the decline of the Compson family.

Dilsey goes to wake the girl, in her usual role of buffer between uncle and niece. Quentin is not in her room, however. Mrs. Compson, certain that her granddaughter has followed in the other Quentin's footsteps, wants to search for a suicide note. Jason, realizing he's been robbed, calls the police.

NOTE: The section is written by an outside observer. Therefore, it contains the descriptions of people and places you get in most novels. Here, in *The Sound and the Fury*'s final section, you learn for the first time what Dilsey and Benjy look like, what Mrs. Compson is wearing, and that the house's front porch is falling down.

Benjy is wailing with unaccustomed force. The sound "might have been all time and injustice and sorrow become vocal for an instant"—a suggestion that Benjy represents a universal condition. (There is also evidence here for those who see Benjy as a Christ figure, suffering for humanity.) Dilsey decides Benjy is smelling what's happening in the house, just as he used to be able to smell death (as you saw in Benjy's and Quentin's sections).

Dilsey, Luster, and Frony take Benjy with them

to church. Frony, more concerned with appearances than her mother, worries what people will think. Dilsey is confident that God doesn't care. In church, the Gibsons (you learn their last name in this section too) hear a powerful sermon about Christ's Resurrection. Dilsey, weeping, realizes that she has seen the final fall of the Compson family. "I seed de beginnin, en now I sees de endin," she tells Frony.

NOTE: Religion   Dilsey's simple but profound religiosity contrasts with the false piety of Mrs. Compson. When Jason is fussing about Quentin, Mrs. Compson complains that this is happening "on Sunday morning, in my own house," when "I've tried so hard to raise them Christians." However, she doesn't go to church on Easter Sunday. Dilsey tells Frony that God doesn't care whether Benjy is smart or not. Dilsey's God is accepting and loving. In contrast, Mrs. Compson says, "Whoever God is, He would not permit that. I'm a lady." Her God observes caste lines. Mrs. Compson makes a point of asking that Dilsey hand her the Bible. Dilsey had previously put it on the bed, but that wasn't good enough for Mrs. Compson, who couldn't be troubled to reach for it. Mrs. Compson uses the Bible to show off how good she is. It isn't an important part of her life, the way it is Dilsey's.

Jason chases after Quentin and the man with the red tie. The sheriff, wondering why Jason kept so much money at home and suspecting whose it was, refuses to accompany him. Jason drives to the town where the show had just moved, almost enjoying the injustice of it all. He bursts into the show trailer, asking where his niece and the man are, and one of the show people knocks him down. (Jason approaches both the sheriff and the show people in the same manner—hostile and aggrieved—and immediately alienates them.) The owner tells him he kicked the man with the red tie out of the show. Jason is forced to hire a young black man to drive him back to Jefferson because his head is injured.

NOTE: Jason and the past The narrator makes clear that Jason's concern was not for his niece or even for the money, but that both represented his revenge for the job he'd been deprived of when Herbert and Caddy broke up. The girl, indeed, was the symbol of the loss of that job. Jason's life since 1911 seems to have been organized around punishing everyone around him for that loss. As the narrator points out, Jason enjoys his anger and his suffering. Why is it that he might be considered as much a prisoner of the past as Benjy or Quentin?

Back at the house, it is impossible to quiet Benjy. He is given the slipper Quentin complained about in Jason's section, and you now realize it must have been Caddy's. But even the slipper is not enough to make him happy. Dilsey allows Luster to take Benjy on the usual Sunday outing to the graveyard. Luster gives him a flower to hold—a broken narcissus, another symbol of the Resurrection (and a damaged one). As they approach the town square, Luster, showing off, turns left around the Confederate monument instead of right, as T.P., who usually drives, always does. Benjy bellows more horrendously than ever. Jason, who has just arrived back in Jefferson, turns the surrey around the right way. As it begins to retrace the route home, Benjy looks out, happy again. For him, everything is now in its ordered place.

NOTE: Some readers point to the pessimism of this ending. Benjy is quieted for a moment, but Jason will soon send him to the asylum. Indeed, despite his defeat by his niece Quentin, Jason takes the reins at the end.

APPENDIX
COMPSON: 1699–1945

By the mid-1940s, many of Faulkner's novels were out of print. This disturbed the literary critic Malcolm Cowley, who was convinced Faulkner was a great writer. Cowley decided to combine extracts from several of Faulkner's works in an anthology. From *The Sound and the Fury*, he chose the fourth section. Cowley asked Faulkner to summarize the three earlier sections of the novel in a few pages so readers of *The Portable Faulkner* (New York: Viking, 1946) would understand what had transpired in them. He complied and the anthology was published in 1946. Later that year, another editor asked Faulkner for an introduction for a new edition of *The Sound and the Fury*. He refused to write one but agreed to let the publisher use the Appendix from the *Portable Faulkner* as an *introduction* to the novel. However, he insisted that it be called an Appendix, not a foreword. In the Vintage Books Edition (New York: Random House, 1954), though, the Appendix was returned to the back of the book.

Within the space of a couple of pages, the Appendix tells the story of the Compson family. It gives the plot of *The Sound and the Fury* and introduces you to the main characters. But it does more than that. It tells you what happened long before Benjy's earliest memory, and it tells you what happened after the novel proper's last scene in 1928. The Appendix almost makes *The Sound and the Fury* a story within a story.

Ikkemotubbe was an Indian chief who owned land in northern Mississippi. He sold a square of it to Jason Compson at just about the time Indians were removed from Mississippi and forced to settle in Oklahoma. Jason was the grandson of Quentin Compson, a Scottish immigrant who settled in Carolina and then in Kentucky. Jason's father, Charles, fought for the British Army in Georgia during the American Revolution but then joined the Americans. Later he participated in an unsuccessful plot to detach the Mississippi Valley from the United States and place it under Spain. After Jason bought the land from Ikkemotubbe, he had an architect build a stately house with formal lawns and white columns. The furniture came by steamboat from France and New Orleans. Jason's son, Quentin II, became governor of Mississippi. Quentin's son, Jason II, was a not very successful Confederate general in the Civil War. He began to sell off the family land, some of it to settlers who came down from New England after the Civil War ended in 1865.

NOTE: Faulkner's myth of the South The beginning of the Appendix contains elements from Faulkner's later novels. The Compsons get their land from an Indian chief who has been unjustly forced from it. The original French settlers of the Indian chief's land called him "l'Homme," or "The Man." The chief picks an English name that sounds similar—Doom. In *Go Down, Moses,* Faulkner wrote that Mississippi was cursed from the start because white men had stolen it from the Indians. The Appendix indicates the Compsons are doomed from the start because the land itself comes from Doom.

Other parts of this story are familiar too. The story of the architect hired to build the big white house and the furniture shipped from France comes from *Absalom, Absalom!* In that novel, too, poor immigrants come to America and one of them sets himself up as an aristocrat. (In *Absalom, Absalom!* his name is Thomas Sutpen, and he is a friend of the Compsons.) But he and the land are doomed, and the dream collapses. In the end, some poor, scrambling people—in other novels, Faulkner calls them the Snopeses—take over. In the Appendix, Faulkner tells you that is beginning to happen by the time General Jason Compson dies in 1900. His grandson, the Jason Compson of *The Sound and the Fury,* will complete the process.

The Compson family's good fortune did not last. Only Jason I and Quentin II lived as true aristocrats. For Faulkner, this tale of poor immigrants who transform themselves into aristocrats but ul-

timately fail and are followed by other poor people
who lack their aristocratic values is the story of the
South.

In the Appendix, Faulkner also links the Compson's story to events in American history. He mentions the American Revolution, President Andrew
Jackson, Daniel Boone, and the Civil War. This
makes the Compsons seem representative of their
region and gives their decline a broader significance.

The Appendix presents in brief the story of *The
Sound and the Fury* and short introductions to its
characters.

The attempt in the Appendix to bring the story
up-to-date is interesting for a number of reasons.
References to Hollywood and World War II place
The Sound and the Fury in the real world, the same
way as earlier references to Andrew Jackson and
Daniel Boone. The mention of Hollywood may have
been a bitter joke by Faulkner, who hated his work
there as a screenwriter. Because both Hollywood
and Nazi Germany are morally corrupt places, it
seems as if Caddy has become more interested in
money than in love. Dilsey won't even look at the
photograph of Caddy with a German general when
the town librarian brings it to her. Dilsey senses
that the Caddy she knew is gone forever.

Jason "held his own with the Snopeses who took
over the little town following the turn of the century as the Compsons . . . faded from it." When
his mother died, he sold the house and committed
his brother to the state asylum. The Appendix also
makes it clear that he stole the support money that

Caddy sent for her daughter and that Quentin took back from him when she ran away. Jason is very happy after his mother dies. Although he never marries, a woman from Memphis in an imitation fur coat comes to visit him every Saturday night. The introductions to Dilsey and her children are brief. Faulkner stresses their strength and the predictability of their lives.

When he talked about *The Sound and the Fury*, Faulkner called the Appendix his final attempt to tell the story of the little girl with the muddy drawers.

In a sense, he was right. The Appendix does summarize the story of *The Sound and the Fury*. It also adds to it, as we have seen. And it takes away from it. The portrait of Quentin in the Appendix is much less complicated than it is in the novel. And Caddy is less interesting and less central.

NOTE: Warning! Faulkner wrote the Appendix without rereading *The Sound and the Fury*. As a result, he got some facts wrong. For example, he says that Luster is fourteen, when he must be at least sixteen or seventeen. And he says that Benjy was castrated in 1913, when the novel suggests that it was 1910.

Do you ever wish you could talk to the author of a book you've just read? Most of the time you can't do that. You can't ask Shakespeare what he really thought of Hamlet. Stephen Crane can't explain the meaning of the red sun in *The Red Badge of Courage*. But William Faulkner gave interviews during the late 1950s and early 1960s, when he was writer-in-residence at the University of Virginia. The transcripts of his conversations with students have been published, as you'll see in the Further Reading section of this guide. There you'll also find listings of other interviews in which Faulkner talked about his work.

Of course, you can't always trust what authors say about what they wrote. Sometimes writers aren't aware of what they've done, or they'd prefer not to talk about their work. William Faulkner liked to pretend that he was just a simple Mississippi farmer. It's true he didn't spend much time in college, but he was a great reader. He may have been a farmer, but he was not a simple man.

In the Appendix, Faulkner is telling you what he thinks the novel meant. The author may not be correct about everything. Make up your own mind about what he says.

A STEP BEYOND

Tests and Answers

TESTS

Test 1

1. The title of *The Sound and the Fury* comes _____
   from Macbeth's speech after
   A. the murder of Banquo
   B. his wife's death
   C. the appearance of the three witches

2. The capital of Faulkner's fictitious Yokna- _____
   patawpha County is
   A. Jackson   B. Oxford
   C. Jefferson

3. Faulkner admired black people for their _____
   A. music   B. hard work
   C. endurance

4. When the golfers yelled "Caddie!" Benjy _____
   Compson thought about how much he
   A. missed the old pasture
   B. missed his sister
   C. wishes he could play golf

5. Luster gets the quarter he needs to go to _____
   the show (to replace the one he lost) from
   A. Quentin   B. Jason   C. Dilsey

6. Jason Compson works in a _____
   A. bank   B. hardware store
   C. drugstore

7. On the morning of his suicide, Quentin _____
   Compson
   I. pulls off the hands of his watch
   II. buys bullets for his gun
   III. walks by the river
   A. I and II only   B. I and III only
   C. II and III only

8. Quentin associates sex with the smell of _____
   A. honeysuckle   B. perfume
   C. whiskey

9. The things that calm Benjy down are _____
   I. an open fire
   II. flowers
   III. Caddy's slipper
   A. I and III only
   B. II and III only
   C. I, II, and III

10. Which of the following is *not* a theme of _____
    The Sound and the Fury?
    A. The decline of a family
    B. The South vs. the North
    C. The past vs. the present

11. Discuss Benjy, Jason, and Quentin as narrators. How
    do their approaches differ? Who is the most reliable?

12. Is *The Sound and the Fury* about the breakup of a
    Southern family, or could it take place anywhere?

13. What makes Benjy bellow? What function does his
    bellowing serve in the novel?

14. What is Dilsey's role in *The Sound and the Fury?*

15. Is the message of this novel that life is "a tale/Told

by an idiot, full of sound and fury,/Signifying nothing"?

Test 2

1. William Faulkner's grandfather was   _____
   A. an Irish immigrant
   B. a major slaveholder
   C. a writer

2. Faulkner told black civil rights leaders to   _____
   A. fight until they won
   B. broaden their appeal to whites
   C. go slow

3. Mrs. Compson believes that the child who   _____
   most resembles her is
   A. Jason   B. Quentin   C. Caddy

4. Faulkner once said that *The Sound and the*   _____
   Fury is the tragedy of two women. He was
   referring to
   A. Caddy and her daughter
   B. Caroline Compson and her daughter
   C. Dilsey Gibson and her daughter

5. When the clock struck five times, Dilsey   _____
   said,
   A. "Git up, Luster"   B. "Five o'clock"
   C. "Eight o'clock"

6. The technique that is not employed in *The*   _____
   Sound and the Fury is
   A. stream-of-consciousness
   B. surrealism
   C. interior monologue

7. At the end of the novel, Benjy is in hyster-   _____
   ics because

    A. he misses Caddy
    B. Jason threatens to send him away
    C. Luster drives around the square the
       wrong way

8. The present action in *The Sound and the Fury* _____
   takes place over the weekend of
   A. Easter   B. Christmas
   C. the Fourth of July

9. The Compson children are playing in the _____
   stream on the night of
   A. the beginning of the Civil War
   B. their grandmother's death
   C. the changing of Benjy's name

10. In the Appendix, Faulkner tells us that after _____
   his mother died, Jason
   A. moved to Memphis
   B. sold the house
   C. got married

11. Why did Faulkner start *The Sound and the Fury* with
   Benjy's section? Should he have?

12. What caused the decline of the Compson family?

13. In the Appendix, Faulkner calls Jason "the first sane
   Compson since before Culloden." Do you agree?

14. What was Faulkner's attitude toward black people?
   Use the characters in this novel to illustrate.

15. Describe Faulkner's attitude toward the past and the
   present, as seen in *The Sound and the Fury*.

ANSWERS

Test 1

1. B   2. C   3. C   4. B   5. A   6. B
7. B   8. A   9. C   10. B

11. Consult the sections Style, Point of View, and Form and Structure in this guide, and review Benjy's, Quentin's, and Jason's sections in the novel. To answer this question, think about what each brother tells you and how he tells it. Consider the limitations of each one. Finally, you will have to decide which gives the most accurate version of events.

Benjy functions as a camera eye, recording what he sees and hears. His section contains simple sentences and a basic vocabulary. He focuses on the distant past, the events of the Compson children's childhood. He is limited by his lack of understanding and by the fact that he was left out of some events.

Quentin's section contains many sentence fragments and a more complicated and abstract vocabulary. He switches between past and present more often than Benjy. He focuses on the events of 1909–1910—Caddy's loss of virginity, her marriage, and the forces leading up to his own suicide. He is limited by his obsession with Caddy's sexuality and by his extreme emotional agitation.

Jason's section is written in everyday speech, although it is slangy, whiny, and a little vulgar. He concentrates on the present, although he also narrates the events of Quentin's and Mr. Compson's deaths. Jason's limitation is his personality. He is mean and dishonest, and sees everything through the lens of how he is taken advantage of (although he usually brings it on himself).

If you think Benjy is the most reliable narrator, you could point to the accuracy of his descriptions as you learn more about events later in the novel. You could say that he is the only Compson brother without an ax to grind. If you think Jason is more accurate, you could point to the comprehensibility of his section. Jason is living in the real world and speaking its language, unlike his brothers. If you think that none of the brothers is thoroughly reliable, you could point to all of their limitations and say that the only way of finding out the truth is to weigh them against each other. (It is almost impossible to make the case that Quentin is the most reliable narrator.)

12. To answer this question, review the sections The Characters and Themes in this guide. Examine the characters of Jason and Caroline Compson and each of their relationships with their children. Look for specific examples to illustrate your points (for example, Mrs. Compson's complaint to Jason that Caddy was always selfish, when we have seen otherwise). Mr. Compson is detached and cynical, while Mrs. Compson is extremely self-centered. Neither gives the children much love or understanding. Caddy makes up for it to some extent, but as she grows up she stops being a mother to her younger brothers, and that adds to their hurt. The children respond to the lack of love in different ways. Caddy becomes promiscuous, Quentin kills himself, and Jason is unhappy and self-defeating.

If you believe that the Compson's story is universal, you would point to the psychological accuracy of these portraits. If you believe that this is a particularly Southern story, you would point to the Appendix, where Faulkner links this story to Southern history.

13. To answer this question, review the The Characters section. Look back, too, at the discussion of Benjy's section in The Story and reread the section in the novel. Try to locate a few representative episodes when Benjy bellows—for example, when the golfers yell "Caddie," when Caddy wears perfume, when Caddy's daughter Quentin runs away, and when Luster drives the wrong way. In all of these cases, Benjy is noticing that things are different and wrong. Some of the other characters, especially Dilsey and her family, say that Benjy can smell death. Benjy's bellowing shows that something is wrong: he has lost something, someone is mistreating him, or something bad is about to happen. His bellowing brings to the novel the feeling of the loss of the past that is one of its most important themes.

14. To answer this question, review the section The Characters and the discussion of Dilsey's section in The Story. Dilsey cooks the meals, cleans the house, raises the children, and keeps Jason and his niece Quentin from killing each other. Her comments (as well as those of Roskus, her husband, and their children), give us a perspective warmer and wiser than that of the Compsons. Dilsey's instinctive kindness toward the Compson children contrasts with the self-centered whining of their mother. And her true Christianity puts Mrs. Compson's false piety to shame. Although Dilsey is not a Compson, she embodies more of the family's original values than do any of the children. And she will endure after the Compson family has disappeared.

15. To answer this question, review the Themes section. Certainly there is evidence in this novel that life is meaningless. Everything seems to be running down, even the clock in the Compson family home. Everything good in the novel dies—Caddy's warmth, Quentin's idealism, even Benjy's sense of being cared for. Caddy apparently becomes the mistress of a Nazi general; Quentin kills himself; Caddy's daughter grows up to be mean and selfish. The final image, of Benjy bellowing, is a horrifying last view of the Compsons. Now the family is in the hands of Jason, who will fire Dilsey, put Benjy away, and turn over the family home to a real estate developer. If you want to argue that life in the novel has meaning, you would have to focus on Dilsey and her family, and the Christian values they embody.

Test 2

1. C   **2.** C   **3.** A   **4.** A   **5.** C   **6.** B
7. C   **8.** A   **9.** B   **10.** B

11. To answer this question, look at the discussions in Style, Point of View, and Form and Structure. You will also want to look at the treatment of Benjy's section in The Story section.

Faulkner began *The Sound and the Fury* with Benjy's section for three logical reasons: (1) Benjy is an idiot, and the passage from which the novel takes its title calls life "a tale/Told by an idiot." (2) To begin the book, Faulkner needed a Compson who was still alive and on the scene in Jefferson in 1928. That left only Benjy, Mrs. Compson, and Jason. Since Jason and Mrs. Compson were both too limited in their perspective, Benjy was the only choice. (3) Benjy mainly thinks about the past, so that his narration is the chronological beginning of the story.

If you think Faulkner made a mistake in putting the Benjy section first, you would point out how difficult it is to make sense of. You would have to show that he should have opened with another section—Jason's or the narrator's—because they are easier to understand.

If you think Faulkner was right in structuring the novel as he did, you would point to the limitations in Jason's point of view. You might also say that the emotional vividness of Benjy's section draws the reader in, as Jason's section would not.

12. To answer this question, review the discussions in the Themes and The Characters sections. You could argue that the decline of the Compson family was caused either by internal psychological problems of the characters or by larger sociological forces. If you want to make the former case, you would closely examine the characters of Mr. and Mrs. Compson. What kind of people were they? How did they relate to their children? You would probably claim that the Compsons were unable to love their children and that the children's problems—Caddy's promiscuity, Quentin's suicide, and Jason's self-defeating nastiness—were all caused by the lack of parental love. If you want to point to larger causes for the problems, you might look to Dilsey and Roskus for explanations. Throughout the novel, Roskus seems to say that the Compson family is cursed.

For a less supernatural explanation, you could turn to Faulkner's Appendix. There he shows that the family decline started with the grandfather who was a Civil War general. All the male Compsons seemed to be affected by grandiose ideals. The original Compson who came to America had been a follower of Bonnie Prince Charlie, a doomed king. Perhaps the decline of the Compson family could be linked prophetically to the original purchase of land from an Indian chief called "Doom."

13. To answer this question, review the discussion of Jason in The Characters and the section on the Appendix in The Story. You will have to describe Jason's character. Do you think he is sane? If so, you would point to his sharp eye for the foibles of the people around him, his sense of humor, and his ability to support what is left of the Compson family. Or you could argue that Faulkner is using the word "sane" in a deprecating or sarcastic way. Jason's values are those of the people around him—and that's awful. If you don't believe that Jason is really sane, you would talk about the way he still acts out his childhood conflicts—his resentments at his brothers and sister, and, in particular, his feeling that Caddy's divorce deprived him of the opportunity to work in Herbert's bank. Jason acts in a self-defeating way. He begins his dealings with both the sheriff and the show people by fighting with them instead of stating his business. Finally, Jason can only have experiences that are based on money. The only relationship he can have with a woman is with a whore.

So one question to decide is whether Jason is sane (and what Faulkner means by that). The other question to answer is about the past Compsons. The Appendix suggests that all the Compsons had bigger dreams than they could carry out. This is true of the original Quentin, and it's even true of the first Jason Compson, who bought the land the family now lives on. And it's true of the grandfather, Jason, the Civil War general who started selling off the land. So there is some question about how truly sane any of the Compson ancestors were. The world of the past may have offered scope for their craziness. The same is not true for Jason Compson IV in 1928.

14. To answer this question, look at The Author and His Times section of this guide as well as the discussion of Dilsey in The Characters and The Story. In life, Faulkner's attitude toward black people was ambivalent. Growing up in a segregated society, Faulkner knew blacks mainly as servants. He admired their strength in suffering and their ability to endure. At the same time, he didn't see black people as the equal of whites. He helped young black people in Oxford, where he lived, to go North for education, but he would not support the civil rights movement. He thought blacks were not ready for full equality and warned civil rights leaders to move slowly.

This attitude is reflected in his portrayal of blacks in *The Sound and the Fury*. Dilsey holds the family together. She is kind, perceptive, and an instinctive Christian. Dilsey embodies the best values of the Compson family, and she will be there after the family is gone.

The fate of Dilsey's family contrasts in some ways with the Compsons. She continues to have good relationships with her children, but her daughter, Frony, is more concerned about public appearances than Dilsey is. And her grandson, Luster, is lazy and mean. The black family may be in decline too.

15. To answer this question, review the section on Themes. The way the characters in *The Sound and the Fury* shift back and forth between the past and the present indicates this is an important theme. One way to compare the past and the present in the novel is to look at Benjy vs. Jason. Benjy is the voice of the past—of the way the family used to be when they were together, listening to the rain in front of the fireplace. Jason is the voice of the present—mean, avaricious, nasty. With Jason, the family will die out.

Except for Dilsey, most of the characters in *The Sound and the Fury* seem to be caught in the past. For Benjy and Quentin, the past is more important than the present. That is partly true of Jason also, because his attitude toward things is so much shaped by his childhood feelings. But Jason is the only member of the Compson family who really knows how to live in and cope with the present.

In general, Faulkner portrays the past more vividly than the present. The past is full of important events. It is also the source of positive family memories and warmth. The present, by contrast, is barren and without values, a reflection, perhaps, of the author's own feelings.

Term Paper Ideas and other Topics for Writing

The Author

1. Faulkner's attitude toward the South.

2. Faulkner and the civil rights movement.

3. Faulkner's attitude toward women.

4. Faulkner and *The Sound and the Fury*—his discussions of the novel in interviews and letters.

5. The place of *The Sound and the Fury* in Faulkner's life work.

Faulkner's Technique

1. Stream-of-consciousness in *The Sound and the Fury*.

2. Multiple narration in *The Sound and the Fury*.

3. The order of the sections—how it works, how it doesn't.

4. Relation between narrative (the plot) and technique.

Themes

1. Religion in *The Sound and the Fury*.

2. The meaning of the past in *The Sound and the Fury*.

3. Faulkner's vision of life in *The Sound and the Fury*.

4. The title quotation from *Macbeth* as a guide to the novel.

Imagery
Trace the following images through the novel and discuss the way they take on meaning.
Clocks/time; shadows; water; honeysuckle.

Benjy
1. Function of Benjy in the novel.

2. Benjy's name change and its role in the novel.

3. Benjy as narrator.

4. Benjy as a Christ figure.

Quentin
1. Meaning of time for Quentin.

2. Quentin's idealism.

3. Quentin's relationship with Mr. Compson.

4. Quentin as a modern hero.

5. Comparison of the character of Quentin in *The Sound and the Fury* and in *Absalom, Absalom!*

Caddy
1. Why doesn't Caddy have a section? Should she? Write some sample pages for a proposed Caddy's section.

2. Mothers and daughters—relations between Mrs. Compson and Caddy, Caddy and Quentin, Dilsey and Frony.

3. Why does Caddy go wrong? Whose fault is it?

Jason
1. Relations between Jason and Mrs. Compson.

2. Why is Jason so angry?

3. Jason's language.

4. Jason as a child.

Dilsey

1. Dilsey as a heroine.

2. Dilsey and the Easter service.

3. Attitude toward blacks in *The Sound and the Fury*.

Theory

1. *The Sound and the Fury* as Christian allegory.

2. *The Sound and the Fury* as psychological allegory.

Further Reading
CRITICAL WORKS

Bleikasten, André. *The Most Splendid Failure: Faulkner's "The Sound and the Fury."* Bloomington: Indiana University Press, 1976.

Blotner, Joseph. *Faulkner: A Biography.* New York: Random House, 1984. This one-volume edition of the definitive Faulkner biography compresses and updates Blotner's original two-volume version, published by Random House in 1974.

———, ed. *Selected Letters of William Faulkner.* New York: Random House, 1977.

Brooks, Cleanth. *William Faulkner: The Yoknapatawpha Country.* New Haven: Yale University Press, 1963.

Cowan, Michael H., ed. *Twentieth Century Interpretations of "The Sound and the Fury."* Englewood Cliffs, N.J.: Prentice-Hall, 1968. A useful collection of critical essays. Contains excerpts from Faulkner's remarks about *The Sound and the Fury,* and essays by Irving Howe, Olga Vickery, Cleanth Brooks, and Carvel Collins.

Cowley, Malcolm. *The Faulkner-Cowley File: Letters and Memories, 1944–1962.* New York: Viking, 1966. The relationship between Faulkner and Cowley, the literary critic responsible for reviving Faulkner's reputation in the 1940s.

———. "Introduction" to *The Portable Faulkner.* New York: Viking, 1946.

Gwynn, Frederick L., and Joseph Blotner, eds. *Faulkner in the University.* Charlottesville: University of Virginia Press, 1959; New York: Random House, Vintage Books, 1965. Faulkner's responses to questions posed by students at the University of Virginia.

Hoffman, Frederick J., and Olga Vickery, eds. *William*

Faulkner: Three Decades of Criticism. New York: Harcourt, Brace, 1963. A fine collection of critical essays.

Howe, Irving. *William Faulkner: A Critical Study.* 3d ed. Chicago: University of Chicago Press, 1975.

Kazin, Alfred. *An American Procession: The Major American Writers from 1830 to 1930.* New York: Knopf, 1984.

Kinney, Arthur F., ed. *Critical Essays on William Faulkner: The Compson Family.* Boston: G. K. Hall, 1982.

Meriwether, James B., and Michael Millgate. *Lion in the Garden: Interviews with William Faulkner, 1926–1962.* New York: Random House, 1968.

Millgate, Michael. *The Achievement of William Faulkner.* Lincoln: University of Nebraska Press, 1978.

Minter, David. *William Faulkner: His Life and Work.* Baltimore: Johns Hopkins University Press, 1980. A lively biography, less complete than Joseph Blotner's but more interpretive.

Peavy, Charles D. *Go Slow Now: Faulkner and the Race Question.* Eugene: University of Oregon Press, 1971. A collection of Faulkner's comments about the American civil rights movement.

Stein, Jean. "William Faulkner." In *Writers at Work: The Paris Review Interviews.* 1st ser., edited by Malcolm Cowley. New York: Penguin Books, 1979. The most revealing interview with Faulkner.

Warren, Robert Penn, ed. *Faulkner: A Collection of Critical Essays.* Englewood Cliffs, N.J.: Prentice-Hall, 1966.

Wilde, Meta Carpenter. *A Loving Gentleman: The Love Story of William Faulkner and Meta Carpenter.* New York: Simon and Schuster, 1976. The story of Faulkner's affair with the author while he was a Hollywood screenwriter.

AUTHOR'S OTHER WORKS

Prose

Soldiers' Pay, 1926.
Mosquitoes, 1927.
Sartoris, 1929.
As I Lay Dying, 1930.
Sanctuary, 1931.
These Thirteen, 1931.
Light in August, 1932.
Doctor Martino and Other Stories, 1934.
Pylon, 1935.
Absalom, Absalom!, 1936.
The Unvanquished, 1938.
The Wild Palms, 1939.
The Hamlet, 1940.
Go Down, Moses and Other Stories, 1942.
Intruder in the Dust, 1948.
Knight's Gambit, 1949.
Collected Stories of William Faulkner, 1950.
Requiem for a Nun, 1951.
A Fable, 1955.
Big Woods, 1955.
The Town, 1957.
The Mansion, 1959.
The Reivers, 1962.
The Wishing Tree, 1964.
Uncollected Stories of William Faulkner, 1979.

Poetry

The Marble Faun, 1924.
A Green Bough, 1933.

Glossary

Apotheosis   Glorified ideal; making a god of a person.

Beale Street   Main street of the black section of Memphis.

Bedlam   An asylum for the mentally ill.

Benjamin   In the Bible, a well-loved youngest son. Traveled to Egypt with his brothers.

Boon/Boone, Daniel, 1734–1820.   A pioneer in Kentucky.

Branch   Brook or stream.

Canaille   Rabble—from a French word meaning "a pack of dogs."

Carpetbagger   Northerner who went South after the Civil War, often to make money.

Culloden Moor   Area in Northwest Scotland; site of a very bloody battle in 1745 when supporters of Bonnie Prince Charles were finally defeated. It signified the defeat of a nation.

Damuddy   Compson children's name for their grandmother.

Dinner   Midday meal.

Drummer   Salesman or commercial traveler.

Gelded   Castrated.

Gelding   One who is castrated, usually used in reference to a horse.

Jackson, Andrew, 1767–1845.   Indian fighter, general, and seventh president of the United States (1829–1837).

Jackson   Capital of Mississippi.

Jason   In Greek mythology, the man who found the Golden Fleece.

Jimson weed   Tall weed with foul-smelling leaves and large white flowers.

Lycurgus   Reformer in seventh-century B.C. Sparta. Planner of a disciplined garrison way of life.

Natural   Idiot.

Non fui. *Sum. Fui. Non sum.*   Latin for: I was not. I am. I was. I am not.

Patrimony   Estate inherited from one's father or other ancestor.

Portico   Covered walkway, usually with columns.

Quai   Landing place, dock.

Reducto absurdum.   *Reductio ad absurdum*—reduction to absurdity. Method of disproving a proposition by showing the absurdity it leads to if carried to its logical conclusion.

Resaca   Civil War battle in May 1864. Confederate General Joseph Johnston temporarily stopped Union General William Sherman's march through Georgia to the sea.

Sarsaparilla   Carbonated beverage. The "sassprilluh" T.P. and Benjy drink at Caddy's wedding is actually champagne.

Sartoris   In Faulkner's novel by the same name, a distinguished Jefferson family, much like the Compsons. Said to have been based on Faulkner's own family.

Sewanee   Town in southeastern Tennessee, site of the University of the South.

Shiloh   Civil War battle in southwestern Tennessee, April 1862; heavy losses on both sides.

Snopeses   Family of poor whites who take over the town of Jefferson from the Compsons and the Sartorises. They appear in many of Faulkner's Yoknapatawpha novels.

Supper   Evening meal.

Surrey   Four-wheeled, two-seated carriage drawn by horses.

Tarleton, Sir Banaster, 1754–1833. British soldier during the American Revolution. Surrendered with
Cornwallis. Known for his cruelty.

Toddy Drink made of spirits (brandy, whiskey, or rum)
and sweetened liquid; usually served hot.

Wilkinson, James, 1757–1825. Military man and ad-
venturer; involved in negotiating Louisiana Purchase
as well as in several schemes.

The Critics

Faulkner on *The Sound and the Fury*

The Sound and the Fury . . . [is] a tragedy of two lost
women: Caddy and her daughter. Dilsey is one of
my own favorite characters, because she is brave,
courageous, gentle, and honest. She's much more
brave and honest and generous than me. . . .

I had already begun to tell the story through the
eyes of the idiot child, since I felt that it would be
more effective as told by someone capable only of
knowing what happened, but not why. I saw that
I had not told the story that time. I tried to tell it
again, the same story through another brother. That
was still not it. I tried to gather the pieces together
and fill in the gaps by making myself the spokes-
man. It was still not complete, not until fifteen years
after the book was published, when I wrote as an
Appendix to another book the final effort to get the
story told and off my mind, so that I myself could
have some peace from it.

—*William Faulkner, quoted in*
Writers at Work, *1979, pp.*
130–31

The Technique of *The Sound and the Fury*

Why has Faulkner broken up the time of his story
and scrambled the pieces? Why is the first window

that opens out on this fictional world the conscious-
ness of an idiot? The reader is tempted to look for
guidemarks and to re-establish the chronology for
himself:

> Jason and Caroline Compson have had three sons
> and a daughter. The daughter, Caddy, has given
> herself to Dalton Ames and become pregnant by
> him. Forced to get hold of a husband quickly . . .

Here the reader stops, for he realizes he is telling
another story. Faulkner did not first conceive this
orderly plot so as to shuffle it afterward like a pack
of cards; he could not tell it any other way. . . . As
soon as we begin to look at any episode, it opens
up to reveal behind it other episodes, all the other
episodes. Nothing happens; the story does not un-
fold; we discover it under each word.

—Jean-Paul Sartre, "On 'The Sound
and the Fury': Time in the Work of
Faulkner," in Robert Penn Warren,
ed., Faulkner: A Collection of
Critical Essays, 1966, p. 87

Christian Symbols

". . . the Compson sons are in parallel with Christ,
but significantly, by inversion. For example, Christ
pleaded to be released from the next day's torture
if such release would not interfere with His Father's
plans, but Quentin pleads with his father for pun-
ishment—which is refused him. When Benjamin is
submerged like Christ on Holy Saturday, he does
not, like Christ, dominate Hell; on the contrary he
is a victim of it. And whereas Holy Saturday is a
time of christening, of name giving, an important
fact about Benjy which is presented in his monologue on Holy Saturday is that *his* name has been
taken away. In short, God's Son passed through the
events of the Passion and rose as a redeemer; the
Compson sons pass through parallel events but go
down in failure. And they do so because love, which

Christ preached as an eleventh commandment, is lacking or frustrated or distorted in their family.

> —*Carvel Collins, "Christian and Freudian Structures," in Michael H. Cowan, ed.,* Twentieth Century Interpretations of "The Sound and the Fury," *1968, p. 73*

Life as a Breakdown

Faulkner's fundamental image [is] life as a perpetual breaking down. In Benjy's mind, the bottommost layer and residue of Compson family history with which the novel opens, the world is all phenomenon, things-are-just happening. . . .

Only as we ascend from Benjy's mind to Quentin's monologue on the day of his death, . . . from Quentin to Jason, the maddened survivor spewing out all his bitterness; from Jason to Faulkner himself, taking over the last section, are we put in the light. . . . But the last word and the last cry out of the book belong not only to Benjy, . . . but to Faulkner's wonderfully sustaining style. The whole book recounts in the most passionate detail life as phenomenon, a descent into breakdown. In the end we are saved and exhilarated by Faulkner's reconstituting all this in the speed and heat of his art.

> —*Alfred Kazin,* An American Procession, *1984*

Signifying Nothing

". . . the theme and the characters are trivial, unworthy of the enormous and complex craftsmanship expended on them. . . . I admit that the idiocy of the thirty-three-year-old Benjy is admirably grasped by Mr. Faulkner, but one hundred pages of an imbecile's simplified sense perceptions and monosyllabic gibberings, no matter how accurately recorded, are too much of a good thing. . . .

. . . After one has penetrated the mad, echoing labyrinth of Mr. Faulkner's style one finds a rather banal Poe-esque plot, a set of degenerate whites whose disintegration is irritating rather than appalling, and two or three Negro characters who, if they were reproduced in straight prose, would appear as fairly conventional types. Sound and fury indeed. Signifying (the witticism is cheap, but inevitable) almost nothing.

—*Clifton P. Fadiman's review of "The Sound and the Fury," in* Arthur F. Kinney, ed., Critical Essays on William Faulkner: The Compson Family, *1982, pp. 92–93*

A Last Word

When Faulkner writes a novel,
  He crowds the symbols in;
There is a hidden meaning
  In every glass of gin.
In every maiden ravished,
  In every colt that's foaled,
And specially in characters
  That are thirty-three years old.

—*John C. Sherwood, in Frederick J. Hoffman and Olga Vickery, eds.,* William Faulkner: Three Decades of Criticism, *1963, p. 35.*